ISSUES THAT CONCERN YOU

Vegetarianism

Jill Hamilton, *Book Editor*

GREENHAVEN PRESS
A part of Gale, Cengage Learning

GALE
CENGAGE Learning

Detroit • New York • San Francisco • New Haven, Conn • Waterville, Maine • London

GALE
CENGAGE Learning™

Christine Nasso, *Publisher*
Elizabeth Des Chenes, *Managing Editor*

LIBRARY OF CONGRESS CATALOGING-IN-PUBLICATION DATA

Vegetarianism / Jill Hamilton, book editor.
  p. cm. — (Issues that concern you)
 Includes bibliographical references and index.
 ISBN-13: 978-0-7377-4188-9 (hardcover) 1. Vegetarianism. 2. Natural foods.
3. Health. I. Hamilton, Jill.
 RM236.V46 2008
 613.2'62—dc22

                                                                    2008019215

Printed in the United States of America
1 2 3 4 5 6 7 13 12 11 10 09

CONTENTS

In the distant past, making food choices was easy—people ate whatever food was available. When and where food became more plentiful, people were able to be more discerning about what they wanted to eat. Personal ethics and preferences guided people's dietary decisions. They still do today, but a host of factors—including technology, farming methods, and environmental issues—make the decision of what to eat much more complex. Moreover, vegetarian and non-vegetarian groups have splintered into countless subgroups that support various specialized eating philosophies.

Technology

The biggest sources of controversy in food production and consumption involve two cutting-edge technologies. The first is cloning, and the latest twist is the January 15, 2008, decision by the Food and Drug Administration to approve the sale of meat and milk from cloned animals. The FDA approval also means that products will not need any special labels saying that they are from cloned animals. Proponents of cloned animals say that the process will allow them to preserve the strongest traits of the best animals through genetic copying. Opponents argue that no long-term studies have been done on the safety of cloned animals and that cloned animals often suffer from unusual health problems. The issue is further complicated when the cloned animals have offspring. If a person does not want to eat meat from a clone, it is likely the clone's offspring would be considered just as unacceptable.

The second major technological controversy in food production is the development of genetically modified organisms (GMOs). GMOs are produced by introducing the genes of one species into the genetic material of another. The idea is to find genes that make a particular plant hardier or more resistant to insects. In

The technological development of genetically modified organisms (GMOs) has raised both hopes for increasing the world's food supply and concerns about contaminating it.

2006 a total of 252 million acres of GMO crops were planted by 10.3 million farmers. The most common genetically modified crops are soybeans, corn, cotton, canola, and alfalfa. Critics of such crops argue that they have not been properly studied and no one knows what, if any, health complications they may bring. People also worry that GMO crops will contaminate unmodified or wild crops (they have been shown to do so) and question the ethics of allowing large companies to "own" a food species and control people's access to it. GMOs raise many eating issues.

The Backlash Against Technology

As large-scale corporate farming has taken over a bigger and bigger share of food production, there has been some consumer backlash. Health scares sweeping the meat industry have caused people to pay closer attention to the practices of big factory farms. Some people, motivated by the conditions in which animals are raised in factory farms, are seeking out organic meat, local meat, or meat raised under humane conditions. One of the newest trends among meat-eaters is a return to an old idea—that animals should be raised on a pasture and fed grass. Grass-fed animals come from smaller-scale operations and produce healthier meat with a lower environmental cost. Even some staunch animal rights advocates support eating meat from such sustainable farms, rather than those from factory farms.

The treatment of animals, such as forced overcrowding on factory farms, presents a serious ethical concern motivating some people to become vegetarian.

People are also looking more carefully at the way our fruits and vegetables are produced. Giant factory farms are monocultures; that is, they have only one type of plant in an area. Monocultures are not healthy for soil; they require more pesticides and fertilizer and they deplete an area of its natural diversity. And, some say, they produce inferior produce. Opponents of factory-farmed produce are quick to note the poor quality of mass-produced tomatoes compared with homegrown ones.

Health-conscious vegetable eaters used to automatically reach for the organically grown produce, but buying organic produce too has become more complicated. A blueberry grown in Chile may be organic, but it also had to be shipped all the way to the local store. The environmental cost of the carbon dioxide produced and the fuel burned to transport the fruit might outweigh the benefits of organic growth. Is it better to stick with organic or is it smarter to choose something from a local grower? What if the local grower does not use pesticides but has not been given an official organic designation?

Many Eating Subgroups

Tricky questions like these have created a number of dietary subgroups based on different eating philosophies. Besides the broad categories of vegetarian and omnivore are vegans, who eat no dairy products or eggs; lacto-ovo vegetarians, who do eat dairy and eggs; and fruitarians, who eat only the ripe fruit of plants and trees. Some people eat meat but choose only organic meat. Others look for meat that is raised under humane conditions. The primary concern for others is to find foods that are produced locally.

Raw food enthusiasts eat only uncooked foods. Freegans look for still-edible discarded and leftover food. In the paleolithic diet, eaters emulate the same diet that our distant cave-dwelling ancestors followed, primarily meat, fish, fruits, vegetables roots, and nuts. Anopsologists follow a type of raw food diet in which they choose foods based on instinct; that is, what smells and tastes best to them.

Diets Are Less Rigid

Ironically, as people splinter into various eating subgroups, there seems to be more acceptance that eating philosophies can be amorphous. Mollie Katzen, author of the popular vegetarian *Moosewood Cookbook*, told a writer for *Food & Wine* magazine that she has been experimenting with meat. "For about 30 years I didn't eat meat at all," she said. "But now that cleaner, naturally fed meat is available, it's a great option for anyone who's looking to complete his diet." Like Katzen, over the course of a lifetime, people may switch between one group and another as their values, health needs, and specific concerns change.

The role of technology in the food debate is just one of the issues related to vegetarianism that students face today. Authors in this anthology examine vegetarianism and other eating philosophies. In addition, the volume contains several appendixes to help the reader understand and explore the topic, including a thorough bibliography and a list of organizations to contact for further information. The appendix "What You Should Know About Vegetarianism" offers facts about food choices and philosophies. The appendix "What You Should Do About Vegetarianism" offers practical tips for young people considering different eating philosophies. With all these features, *Issues That Concern You: Vegetarianism* provides an excellent resource for everyone interested in this issue.

ONE

Anatomy Offers Few Clues as to What the Human Diet Should Be

Sally Deneen

In the following article, Seattle-based writer Sally Deneen looks to human anatomy for the answer to the question of whether humans are biologically designed to be vegetarians or omnivores. While some experts point to the ways in which humans resemble vegetarian animals—such as intestinal tract length and relative mouth size—others note that humans do not have multiple stomachs like many herbivores. Although anatomy makes it clear that humans are not meant to be entirely carnivorous, biology offers only partial evidence of what our diet should be. Deneen is a frequent contributor to *E: The Environmental Magazine*.

Cardiologist William C. Roberts hails from the famed cattle state of Texas, but he says this without hesitation: Humans aren't physiologically designed to eat meat. "I think the evidence is pretty clear. If you look at various characteristics of carnivores versus herbivores, it doesn't take a genius to see where humans line up," says Roberts, editor in chief of *The American Journal of Cardiology* and medical director of the Baylor Heart and Vascular Institute at Baylor University Medical Center in Dallas.

As further evidence, Roberts cites the carnivore's short intestinal tract, which reaches about three times its body length. An herbivore's intestines are 12 times its body length, and humans are closer to herbivores, he says. Roberts rattles off other similarities between human beings and herbivores. Both get vitamin C from their diets (carnivores make it internally). Both sip water, not lap it up with their tongues. Both cool their bodies by perspiring (carnivores pant).

Human beings and herbivorous animals have little mouths in relation to their head sizes, unlike carnivores, whose big mouths are all the better for "seizing, killing and dismembering prey," argues nutrition specialist Dr. Milton R. Mills, associate director of preventive medicine for the Washington, D.C.–based Physicians Committee for Responsible Medicine (PCRM).

What Teeth Tell About Diet

Incisors

Carnivore	Short and pointed
Herbivore	Broad, flattened, and spade-shaped
Omnivore	Short and pointed
Human	Broad, flattened, and spade-shaped

Canines

Carnivore	Long, sharp, and curved
Herbivore	Dull and short or long (for defense), or none
Omnivore	Long, sharp, and curved
Human	Short and blunted

Molars

Carnivore	Sharp, jagged, and blade-shaped
Herbivore	Flattened with cusps vs. complex surface
Omnivore	Sharp blades and/or flattened
Human	Flattened with nodular cusps

Taken from: Milton R. Mills, MD, "The Comparative Anatomy of Eating," Earthsave Canada. www.earthsave.ca/articles/health/comparative.html.

People and herbivores extensively chew their food, he says, whereas swallowing food whole is the preferred method of carnivores and omnivores.

Humans and Dairy

Dr. Neal D. Barnard, PCRM's founder and president, says humans lack the raw abilities to be good hunters. "We are not quick, like cats, hawks or other predators," he says. "It was not until the advent of arrowheads, hatchets and other implements that killing and capturing prey became possible."

Milk, another animal product, can also be problematic for people. That's why, in response to the popular "Got Milk?" ad campaign, Barnard's organization sponsored billboards this past summer [in 2001] that read, "Got Diarrhea?"

"Dairy foods are definitely not a natural part of our diet," contends vegetarian dietitian and author Virginia Messina, who fields the public's nutritional questions at www.VegRD.com. "We only started consuming them about 10,000 years ago, which is very recent in our evolution. Our physiology suggests that we really did not evolve to consume dairy beyond early childhood."

Three out of 10 adults are lactose intolerant, meaning they can't digest the sugar in milk. So they likely suffer gas or diarrhea when undigested lactose reaches the large intestine, according to an April [2001] report in the Nutrition Action Healthletter.

While celebrities sport milk mustaches in ad campaigns, some research raises questions as to whether milk is a better source of calcium than, say, spinach or collard greens. Echoing the conclusions of research elsewhere, a Harvard University study of more than 75,000 nurses found no evidence that nurses who drank the most milk enjoyed fewer broken bones.

Milk's high protein actually could leach calcium from bones, according to Dr. Walter Willett, of the Harvard School of Public Health, speaking on the PBS program HealthWeek. "Drinking cow milk has been linked to iron-deficiency anemia in infants and children; it has been named as the cause of cramps and diarrhea in much of the world's population and the cause of multiple

Some believe that the resemblance between humans and herbivores is suggested by the length of the intenstines, but the human lack of multiple stomachs points to the need for a more diverse diet.

forms of allergies as well. The possibility has been raised that it may play a central role in the origins of atherosclerosis and heart attacks," writes Dr. Frank Oski, former director of the Johns Hopkins University Department of Pediatrics, in his book, *Don't Drink Your Milk!*

Human Physiology Is Mixed

As intriguing as these arguments may be, the idea that humans are natural vegetarians has "no scientific basis in fact," argues anatomist and primatologist John McArdle. Alarmed by this growing belief, McArdle, a vegetarian, says the human anatomy proves that people are omnivores. "We obviously are not carnivores, but we are equally obviously not strict vegetarians, if you carefully examine the anatomical, physiological and fossil evidence," says McArdle, executive director of the Alternatives Research and

Development Foundation in Eden Prairie, Minnesota. According to a 1999 article in the journal the *Ecologist*, several of our physiological features "clearly indicate a design" for eating meat, including "our stomach's production of hydrochloric acid, something not found in herbivores. Furthermore, the human pancreas manufactures a full range of digestive enzymes to handle a wide variety of foods, both animal and vegetable.

"While humans may have longer intestines than animal carnivores, they are not as long as herbivores; nor do we possess multiple stomachs like many herbivores, nor do we chew cud," the magazine adds. "Our physiology definitely indicates a mixed feeder." If people were designed to be strict vegetarians, McArdle expects we would have a specialized colon, specialized teeth and a stomach that doesn't have a generalized pH—all the better to handle roughage. Tom Billings, a vegetarian for three decades and site editor of BeyondVeg.com, believes humans are natural omnivores. Helping prove it, he says, is the fact that people have a low synthesis rate of the fatty acid DHA and of taurine, suggesting our early ancestors relied on animal foods to get these nutrients. Vitamin B_{12}, also, isn't reliably found in plants. That, Billings says, left "animal foods as the reliable source during evolution."

Historically Humans Have Been Omnivores

History argues in favor of the omnivore argument, considering that humans have eaten meat for 2.5 million years or more, according to fossil evidence. Indeed, when researchers examined the chemical makeup of the teeth of an early African hominid that lived in woodlands three million years ago, they expected to learn that our ancestor lived on fruits and leaves. "But the isotopic clues show that it ate a varied diet, including either grassland plants or animals that themselves fed on grasses," reported the journal *Science* in 1999.

So, the question remains: Are humans natural vegetarians? In the end, whether a person lives a vegetarian lifestyle has less to do with esoteric matters of anatomy and more to do with ethics and personal values. The architecture of the human body offers no simple answers.

TWO

A Vegetarian Diet Is Key to Good Health

Physicians Committee for Responsible Medicine Nutrition Staff

> The following essay from the Physicians Committee for Responsible Medicine advocates a vegetarian diet for good health. The authors outline the health benefits of a vegetarian or vegan diet, such as a reduced risk of cancer and better heart health. They also suggest special dietary considerations for vegetarians and offer tips on how to begin a vegetarian diet. The Washington, D.C., nonprofit PCRM describes itself as "an organization of doctors and laypersons working together for compassionate and effective medical practice, research and health promotion."

A vegetarian menu is a powerful and pleasurable way to achieve good health. The vegetarian eating pattern is based on a wide variety of foods that are satisfying, delicious, and healthful.

Vegetarians avoid meat, fish, and poultry. Those who include dairy products and eggs in their diets are called lacto-ovo vegetarians. Vegans (pure vegetarians) eat no meat, fish, poultry, eggs, or dairy products. While there is a considerable advantage to a lacto-ovo vegetarian pattern, vegan diets are the healthiest of all, reducing risk of a broad range of health concerns.

Physicians Committee for Responsible Medicine, "Vegetarian Starter Kit; Vegetarian Foods: Powerful Tools for Health," May 2, 2005. Reproduced by permission.

The Health Benefits

Vegetarians have much lower cholesterol levels than meat-eaters, and heart disease is less common in vegetarians. The reasons are not hard to find. Vegetarian meals are typically low in saturated fat and usually contain little or no cholesterol. Since cholesterol is found only in animal products such as meat, dairy, and eggs, vegans consume a cholesterol-free diet.

The type of protein in a vegetarian diet may be another important advantage. Many studies show that replacing animal protein with plant protein lowers blood cholesterol levels—even if the amount and type of fat in the diet stays the same. Those studies show that a low-fat, vegetarian diet has a clear advantage over other diets.

An impressive number of studies, dating back to the early 1920s, show that vegetarians have lower blood pressure than nonvegetarians. In fact, some studies have shown that adding meat to a vegetarian diet raises blood pressure levels rapidly and significantly. The effects of a vegetarian diet occur in addition to the benefits of reducing the sodium content of the diet. When patients with high blood pressure begin a vegetarian diet, many are able to eliminate the need for medication.

The latest studies on diabetes show that a vegetarian diet high in complex carbohydrates and fiber (which are found only in plant foods) and low in fat is the best dietary prescription for controlling diabetes. A diet based on vegetables, legumes, fruits, and whole grains, which is also low in fat and sugar, can lower blood sugar levels and often reduce or even eliminate the need for medication. Since individuals with diabetes are at high risk for heart disease, avoiding fat and cholesterol is important, and a vegetarian diet is the best way to do that.

Vegetarian Diets Help Prevent Cancer

A vegetarian diet helps prevent cancer. Studies of vegetarians show that death rates from cancer are only about one-half to three-quarters of the general population's death rates. Breast cancer rates are dramatically lower in countries where diets are

A number of studies show that death rates from cancer and heart disease are lower among vegetarians and in countries with plant-based diets.

typically plant-based. When people from those countries adopt a Western, meat-based diet, their rates of breast cancer soar. Vegetarians also have significantly lower rates of colon cancer than meat-eaters. Colon cancer is more closely associated with meat consumption than any other dietary factor.

Why do vegetarian diets help protect against cancer? First, they are lower in fat and higher in fiber than meat-based diets. But other factors are important, too. Plants contain other cancer-fighting substances called phytochemicals. For example, vegetarians usually consume more of the plant pigments beta-carotene and lycopene. This might help to explain why they have less lung and prostate cancer. Also, some studies have suggested that diets that avoid dairy products may reduce the risk of prostate and ovarian cancer.

Some of the anti-cancer aspects of a vegetarian diet cannot yet be explained. For example, researchers are not quite sure why vegetarians have more of certain white blood cells, called "natural killer cells," which are able to seek out and destroy cancer cells.

Vegetarians are less likely to form either kidney stones or gallstones. In addition, vegetarians may also be at lower risk for osteoporosis because they eat little or no animal protein. A high intake of animal protein encourages the loss of calcium from the bones. Replacing animal products with plant foods reduces the amount of calcium lost. This may help to explain why people who live in countries where the diet is typically plant-based have little osteoporosis, even when calcium intake is lower than that in dairy-consuming countries.

Planning a Nutritious Vegetarian Diet

It's easy to plan vegetarian diets that meet all your nutrient needs. Grains, beans, and vegetables are rich in protein and iron. Green leafy vegetables, beans, lentils, tofu, corn tortillas, and nuts are excellent sources of calcium, as are enriched soymilk and fortified juices.

Vitamin D is normally made in the body when sun shines on the skin. People who are dark-skinned or live at northern latitudes have some difficulty producing vitamin D year-round. Vitamin D can easily be obtained from fortified foods. Some sources are commercial breakfast cereals, soymilk, other supplemental products, and multivitamins.

Regular intake of vitamin B_{12} is important. Good sources include all common multiple vitamins (including vegetarian vitamins), fortified cereals, some brands of nutritional yeast, and fortified soymilk. It is especially important for pregnant women and breast-feeding mothers to get enough vitamin B12.

When reading food labels, look for the word cyanocobalamin in the ingredient list. This is the form of vitamin B12 that is best absorbed. . . .

How to Switch to a Vegetarian Diet

If you are making the switch to a vegetarian diet for its health benefits, you'll be pleased to find that there is a wonderful additional benefit to vegetarian eating: It's a delicious and fun way to explore new foods. A vegetarian meal can be as familiar as spaghetti with

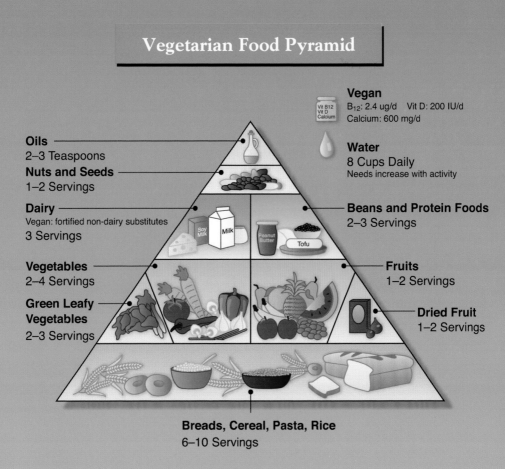

Vegetarian Food Pyramid

Oils
2–3 Teaspoons

Nuts and Seeds
1–2 Servings

Dairy
Vegan: fortified non-dairy substitutes
3 Servings

Vegetables
2–4 Servings

**Green Leafy
Vegetables**
2–3 Servings

Vegan
B12: 2.4 ug/d   Vit D: 200 IU/d
Calcium: 600 mg/d

Water
8 Cups Daily
Needs increase with activity

Beans and Protein Foods
2–3 Servings

Fruits
1–2 Servings

Dried Fruit
1–2 Servings

Breads, Cereal, Pasta, Rice
6–10 Servings

Taken from: Department of Nutrition, Arizona State University, 2002.

marinara sauce, as comforting as a bowl of rich, potato soup, or as exotic as Grilled Polenta with Portabella Mushrooms.

The switch to a vegetarian diet is easier than you might think. Most people, whether vegetarians or meat-eaters, typically use a limited variety of recipes; the average family eats only eight or nine different dinners repeatedly. You can use a simple, three-step method to come up with nine vegetarian dinner menus that you enjoy and can prepare easily.

1. First, think of three vegetarian meals that you already enjoy. Common ones are tofu and vegetable stir-fry, vegetable stew, or pasta primavera.

2. Second, think of three recipes that you prepare regularly that can easily be adapted to a vegetarian menu. For example, a favorite chili recipe can be made with all of the same ingredients; just replace the meat with beans or texturized vegetable protein. Enjoy bean burritos (using canned vegetarian refried beans) instead of beef burritos, veggie burgers instead of hamburgers, and grilled eggplant and roasted red peppers instead of grilled chicken in sandwiches. Many soups, stews, and casseroles also can be made into vegetarian dishes with a few simple changes.

3. Third, check out some vegetarian cookbooks from the library and experiment with the recipes for a week or so until you find three new recipes that are delicious and easy to make. Just like that, with minimal changes to your menus, you will have nine vegetarian dinners.

Vegetarian Breakfasts and Lunches

After that, coming up with vegetarian options for breakfast and lunch is easy. Try muffins with fruit spread, cholesterol-free French toast, or cereal for breakfasts. Sandwiches, with spreads like hummus or white bean pate with lemon and garlic, or dinner leftovers all make great lunches.

THREE

Teen Vegetarians Need to Be Aware of Nutrition Pitfalls

Kindy R. Peaslee

In the following essay, registered dietitian Kindy R. Peaslee writes about the increase in teens who choose a vegetarian diet and the kinds of challenges they face. Some meat-eating families do not support the teen's choice. Some peers may not understand why friends would deprive themselves of certain foods. Teens also need to understand that simply giving up meat does not mean their diet is healthy. A diet of sugary and fatty snack foods is less healthy than one that contains meat. Peaslee is the founder of a marketing firm committed to "increasing wellness thinking."

Jessica is a competitive runner. She watches what she eats and tries to keep her weight down to help her speed. One night at dinner, when her mother passes the chicken, Jessica says, "No thanks, I've decided to become a vegetarian." Her mother isn't quite sure how to respond and wonders whether Jessica is only trying to legitimize the exclusion of additional foods from her diet.

Since Paul started middle school, he has been withdrawing from his family in different ways. His family is largely meat and potato eaters; thus, his parents are not pleased when Paul decides to become a vegetarian. His father believes Paul is rejecting their family's way of eating. Paul's mother is concerned about the

Kindy R. Peaslee, RD, "Raising a Healthy Vegetarian Teen," *Today's Dietitian*, vol. 8, February 2006, p. 58. Reproduced by permission.

adequacy of his diet, since he is excluding many foods without adding nutritionally equivalent substitutes. She also misses Paul at family meals; he says there's not much point in joining the family because they eat foods he can't eat and seeing meat on the table bothers him.

These real-life scenarios of vegetarian teenagers are shared by author and researcher Dianne Neumark-Sztainer, PhD, MPH, RD, in her new book *"I'm, Like, SO Fat!": Helping Your Teen Make Healthy Choices About Eating and Exercise in a Weight-Obsessed World*. After conducting one of the largest and most comprehensive studies on eating patterns and weight-related issues in adolescents, Neumark-Sztainer knows how American teenagers eat. Called Project EAT (Eating Among Teens), the University

Fordham University students can select from international dishes and even vegan meals in the school's cafeterias.

of Minnesota study was designed to track eating patterns, physical activity, dieting behaviors, and weight concerns of 4,746 adolescents and 900 parents.

Vegetarianism Goes Mainstream

Vegetarianism has become a booming nutrition trend over the past few years. Now more than ever, vegetarian families are bringing this once-alternative dietary choice to the attention of mainstream America. Evidence of the progress is everywhere: McDonald's now offers an array of meatless salads; school lunch programs now offer vegetarian entrees; and meat alternatives, such as tofu, are sold in most supermarkets.

Taking a stand for animal rights by choosing not to eat meat fits well with teenagers wanting to be part of a cause. As they try to sort through their own philosophies on avoiding meat, poultry, or fish, teens may use their newfound food beliefs as a platform to further separate themselves from concerned family members. Many of these teens are looking out for the animal's health but ironically can easily neglect their own health in the process.

How Many Teens Are Vegetarian?

In 2000, the Vegetarian Resource Group (VRG), a nonprofit group working to educate people about vegetarianism and related issues, conducted a Roper poll on 1,240 youths to track the number of young vegetarians in the United States. They found that 2% of youth aged 6 to 17 never eat meat, fish, or poultry.

More recently, Project EAT found a 4% increase from the Roper poll results, showing that a total of 6% of the teens surveyed said they were vegetarians. The study also found that the first step many teens take on their way to becoming vegetarians is to eliminate red meat from their diet.

Reed Mangels, PhD, RD, coauthor of the American Dietetic Association's position paper on vegetarianism and nutrition advisor for the VRG, gives feedback on why teens are choosing to become vegetarian. "In my experience, teens become vegetarian because of concerns about animals, the environment, health reasons, and a desire to emulate a peer or a celebrity," she comments. "I do not feel that more teens are becoming vegetarian because of body image or weight issues than are becoming vegetarian for environmental or animal issues."

Concerned Parents

So what do parents need to know if they want to raise children on a meatless diet or if a child suddenly announces that he or she is now a vegetarian? To start, parents must be aware of the nutritional needs teenage vegetarians have and how to creatively inspire their teenagers to eat a variety of foods. Finding healthy foods their children genuinely enjoy can go a long way toward ensuring that their children's nutritional needs are being met. Nutrients that are usually supplied by meat, dairy, and egg products must be worked back into a teen's diet to meet the recommended dietary allowance for protein, calcium, iron, and vitamin B_{12}.

How concerned are mothers who are already vegetarian? A mother of three and a vegetarian for more than 17 years, Naomi Arens says she would not mind if her children chose a vegetarian diet. She has decided to let her children choose for themselves whether they will avoid meat. "As a mom, my main concern is that my [children's] diets are not always the most healthful or balanced. . . . To eliminate a major food group might make it more difficult," says Arens. "My kids like lots of vegetarian foods, such as tofu, so they would probably do fine." She admits that in a "fast-food world," though, eating vegetarian takes more time and planning, which she believes could be difficult for busy families making the switch.

Mangels and her husband are both vegan. "We weren't going to do anything different for the kids," she says. "We tend to be a little loose in social situations and tell our daughters when something is likely to contain eggs and allow them to decide whether to eat it." What her children do eat are beans—veggie baked beans, bean burritos, and beans and rice—and hot dogs and hamburgers made with tofu or other meat substitutes for protein. Fortified juices,

Vegetarian Food Guide for Teens

Food Group	Servings per Day	Serving Size	Comments
Bread, rice, cereal, and pasta	6–7 or more	1 slice of bread or ½ bagel 1 ounce ready-to-eat cereal ½ C. rice, pasta, or grain 4 graham crackers 8 crackers	Choose whole grain breads and cereals. Choose fortified grain breads and cereals.
Legumes, eggs, and meat substitutes	2 or more	½ C. beans, peas, lentils ½ C. tofu, tempeh, textured vegetable protein, soy protein, or meat analogs	These provide iron, zinc, and other nutrients as well as protein. Eggs provide vitamin B_{12}.
Fruits and vegetables	5 or more	½ C. cooked or canned fruit or vegetable 1 C. raw vegetable 1 piece of fruit ½-¾ C. fruit juice	Eat a variety of fruits and vegetables. Juices don't provide fiber as do whole foods. Include leafy greens daily.
Nuts and seeds	1 or more	¼ C. nuts or seeds 2 T. peanut butter or tahini	Flax seed (ground) and walnuts provide α-linolenic acid (essential fatty acid).
Fats and oils	6 or more	1 tsp. oil or margarine 2 tsp. salad dressing	Soybean, canola, walnut, and flaxseed oils are rich in α-linolenic acid (essential fatty acid).
Milk or milk alternatives	3–4	1 C. milk or yogurt 1 C. fortified soy or rice milk 1½ oz. (⅓ C.) cheese 1 C. pudding 1½ oz. ice milk or frozen yogurt	Choose low-fat or non-fat dairy products. Choose milk substitutes fortified with calcium, vitamin D, and vitamin B_{12}.

Taken from: P. Johnston, E. Haddad, "Vegetarian Diets and Pregnant Teens," in M. Story, J. Stang, eds., *Nutrition and the Pregnant Adolescent: a Practical Reference Guide.* Minneapolis, MN: Center for Leadership, Education and Training in Maternal and Child Nutrition, Division of Epidemiology, University of Minnesota, 2000. www.epiumn.edu/let/pubs/nmpa.shtm.

soy milk, and supplements provide calcium; one daughter also gets calcium from collards, kale, and broccoli, which the other daughter doesn't like.

Family Communication Is Key

Communication between parents and teens and the example the parents set matter tremendously. The key to understanding why your child is bent toward this new way of eating is effective communication. Teens watch and listen to their parents, in addition to other influencers such as friends, media, and the Internet. Parents need to stay alert and be aware of their own food-related and body image issues and the messages they are sending to their children. Project EAT found that teens whose parents reported eating more fruits, vegetables, and dairy foods were also more likely to eat more of these foods.

Compromise is the best way for a "nonvegetarian" family to adapt to a vegetarian teen. Parents should develop a plan to include the teen in food preparation or grocery shopping. Don't change everything—your new vegetarian still needs to come to family meals and take the responsibility for the time it takes to eat and plan vegetarian meals.

If parents are worried about their teenager's nutritional needs, a diet recall will help determine whether the teen's diet is low in some areas, such as vitamins or iron, and supplements can be added to the diet. Parents can take advantage of their child's vegetarian focus by weaving in lessons on nutrition. To many teens, vegetarianism seems like the "right" or noble thing to do. But do they understand the different types of vegetarian diets and the effort it will take to add meat alternatives back into their diets?

According to Project EAT, the most common reason in choosing to not eat meat was to maintain or lose weight. Vegans were not as interested in weight control issues. Lee Kaufman says she did not decide to become a vegetarian as an 18-year-old for body image reasons. Rather, her decision was founded entirely in her ethical beliefs. Kaufman quips, "If it didn't come from a cow, I would love a steak right now!"

Neumark-Sztainer believes that vegetarianism leading to an eating disorder is the exception rather than the rule. She says that those who are already on their way to developing disordered eating behaviors may adopt vegetarianism as an additional strategy for restricting food intake. Ilyse Simon, RD, a private practitioner specializing in disordered eating, agrees, commenting that some of the young girls she counsels who are anorexic have become vegetarians because they kept restricting their food intake.

Vegetarian Teens Need Special Support

It is estimated that teenagers may be the fastest-growing group of vegetarians and often require special resources and support when their families aren't supportive of their dietary choice. Lack of proper nutrition can cause teenage vegetarians to become protein malnourished since the meat is removed from the meal mix. And many teens do not realize that just because a vegetarian diet is lower in fat intake, it doesn't mean it is lower in calories, especially when sugary desserts and snack foods are chosen.

Another danger is a lack of emotional support, either from parents or peers who may not understand the decision. Even when a teen wants to be a vegetarian, it can still be difficult. Kevin Cummings, a vegetarian since the age of 12 and now in his late 20s, remembers how hard it was in middle and high school—specifically, dealing with ridicule about his vegetarian diet. Sasha Clark, a 16-year-old vegan since birth, says, "The worst part of being vegan used to be the teasing that I got, and some people 'pitied' me because I couldn't eat what they ate. But now that I'm older, I try to use these moments as educational opportunities." Clark was interviewed by VegFamily on her story of living as a vegan teen. "Today, though," she says, "I am happy to say that the best part of being vegan is knowing that my diet is contributing not only to my health but also to the well-being of animals and to the good of the environment."

Teens Need Healthy Vegetarian Snacks and Meal Ideas

When a vegetarian teen is in the house, it's time to get creative with the snack list. Have the house stocked with trail mix, popcorn, pizza, bean tacos, bagels, and dried fruits to keep the "ultimate teen snacker" eating well throughout the day with at least four to five mini-meals. Eating out is easier than ever before for vegetarian teens with the presence of Mexican food chains and many local Chinese, Japanese, and Mediterranean restaurants.

Most dietitians I spoke with who have teenage vegetarian clients agree that teens avoiding meat is becoming a trend or fad and that the vegetarian teenagers (mostly girls aged 14 to 17) they counsel usually come from meat-eating families. Kathryn Fink, RD, a private practitioner in Texas, mentioned, "Many of the teens are uneducated about being vegetarian and the essential nutrients they need to obtain. I explain the complementary proteins and work with them on understanding the nutrients that will help their bodies to be healthy and grow into young adults."

FOUR

It Is Possible to Be a Conscientious Carnivore

Tamar Haspel

"Until relatively recently, when grass-fed beef and free-roaming pork began arriving in stores," writes Tamar Haspel in the following article, "consumers had to be one of three things: carnivore, vegetarian or hypocrite." Haspel writes that sustainable agriculture offers a third way: being a conscientious carnivore. Small farmers using humane and sustainable techniques such as letting animals roam free give the animal a better life and offer benefits to the environment. Sustainable agriculture also lets meat-eaters consume free-range chickens with less guilt. Haspel is a food and health writer.

It's almost a movement. Sustainable agriculture—David to factory farming's Goliath—is capturing the eating public's imagination with its contented cows, bucolic landscape and its practice of leaving the environment intact.

With an assist from some recent books describing the miserable lives of animals under big agriculture, the small farmer's message that we should care about the lives of our livestock is getting traction. As it does, it gives those of us with a concern for animals, but also a fondness for pork chops, a place to hang our hats.

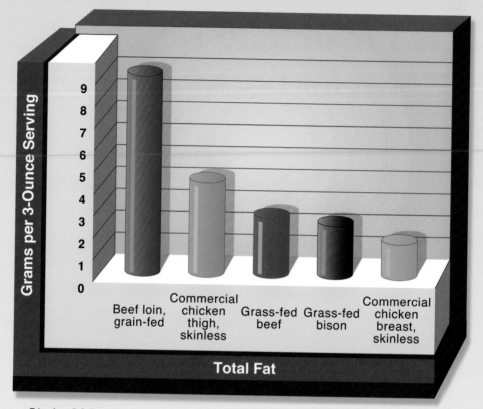

Fat in Grass-fed Meat Versus Commercial Meat

Grams per 3-Ounce Serving

9
8
7
6
5
4
3
2
1
0

Beef loin, grain-fed | Commercial chicken thigh, skinless | Grass-fed beef | Grass-fed bison | Commercial chicken breast, skinless

Total Fat

Taken from: D.C. Rule et al., "Comparison of Muscle Fatty Acid Profiles and Cholesterol Concentrations of Bison, Beef Cattle, Elk, and Chicken," *Journal of Animal Science*, no. 5, 2002.

Until relatively recently, when grass-fed beef and free-roaming pork began arriving in stores, consumers had to be one of three things: carnivore, vegetarian or hypocrite. If you didn't care about your pork chop's quality of life, you could be a carnivore. If you did, you could either renounce it and be a vegetarian or eat it anyway and, well . . . .

Vegetarians had a good claim to the ethical and environmental high ground. Factory farms abuse animals and devastate the environment, and a world where we all eat plants is clearly better than that. When you put the vegetarian vision up against a system of small, sustainable farms, though, the equation changes.

Ecologically, vegetarians focus on efficiency. If humans eat animals that eat plants, it takes much more land to feed us than if humans just eat the plants. That seems like a quaint concern, though, in this era of abundance. Besides, what would we put on freed-up farmland? Gated communities? Wal-Mart?

Animals Help in Sustainability

There's also more to agriculture than efficiency. If animals make farming less efficient, they also act as weed control, pest control and fertilizer while they do it—they're integral to sustainability. Michael Pollan, in *The Omnivore's Dilemma*, profiles Polyface Farm, where the cows and chickens make the lettuce and sweet corn possible. And Joel Salatin, the farm's owner, makes a different kind of efficiency argument: Animals convert calories that human can't eat (such as grass) or prefer not to eat (such as grubs) into calories humans want to eat (such as chicken).

None of this would matter if the livestock suffered. Sustainability couldn't excuse keeping pigs in such close confinement that they chewed each other's tails off. But the beauty of the sustainable farm is that the pigs root, roam and wallow. Of course, you still have to kill them, and there are people who find that unacceptable under any circumstances.

Ethical Meat-Eating

But there's a strong case that giving a farm animal a happy life, making a constructive environmental contribution, and slaughtering it humanely to feed people is ethical. Even animal rights hard-liner Peter Singer, in *The Way We Eat* (co-authored with Jim Mason), can't condemn "the view that it is ethical to eat animals who have lived good lives and would not have existed at all." He concludes that it's "more appropriate to praise" this relatively enlightened view than to criticize it for not being the veganism he prefers.

Vegetarians have one more motivation: health. While vegetarians are undoubtedly healthier than meat eaters, no study has compared a wholly vegetarian diet to a largely vegetarian diet that includes some grass-fed beef, free-rooting pork or cage-less poultry. Since grass-fed meat provides some nutrients missing from vegetarian diets (long-chain omega-3 fats, for example), it's just possible that vegetarians might be better off eating a little meat. We don't know. (The real health benefit of eating sustainably, though, might be decreased meat consumption among carnivores—a response to the higher price of grass-fed meat.)

And so we can have the moral high ground and the pork chop. But the point here isn't to holier-than-thou the vegetarians (all of the sanctimony, none of the tofu!). By eating only animals that are raised sustainably and treated well—and those in moderation—we can protect our environment, our livestock and our

The Reverend Jeffrey Hawkins teaches about sustainable agriculture—farming that endeavors to give animals both a healthy environment and a chance to contribute to sustaining the environment of the farm.

health and support the small, sustainable farms that might be able to change the nature of American agriculture.

A vegetarian alternative needs a name. Singer suggests "conscientious omnivore," which, while accurate, doesn't exactly trip off the tongue. Since we're shifting the emphasis from what we eat to how what we eat was raised, how about "farmivore"? And, since every good movement needs a motto: Eat the farm.

FIVE

There Is No Such Thing as Guilt-Free Meat

Colleen Patrick-Goudreau

> In the following selection, chef and animal activist Colleen Patrick-Goudreau argues that animal products marketed with terms like "humanely raised," "free range," and "sustainable" are not as guilt-free as they sound. "The movement toward 'humanely raised food animals' simply assuages our guilt more than it actually reduces animal suffering," she writes. She details some of the lesser known, less humane-sounding aspects of the meat industry such as the practice of artificially inseminating "natural" turkeys because their breasts are so large that they are unable to mate in the normal way. She also points out that, regardless of the quality of an animal's life, by law if it is destined for a dinner table it must be killed in a USDA-certified slaughterhouse. Patrick-Goudreau founded Compassionate Cooks, an organization founded to educate people about animal rights and the benefits of vegetarian diets. She is the author of *The Joy of Vegan Baking*.

I have yet to meet a non-vegetarian who didn't care about the treatment of animals raised and killed for human consumption. Even people who eat meat, aware on some level that the experience is unpleasant for the animals, will tell you they object to

Colleen Patrick-Goudreau, "From Cradle to Grave," Common Dreams.org, October 31, 2006. Reproduced by permission of the author.

unnecessary abuse and cruelty. They declare that they buy only "humane" meat, "free-range" eggs and "organic" milk, perceiving themselves as ethical consumers and these products as the final frontier in the fight against animal cruelty. Though we kill over 10 billion land animals every year to please our palates, we never question the absurdity of this sacred societal ritual. Instead, we absolve ourselves by making what we think are guilt-free choices, failing to recognize the paradox of "humane slaughter" and never really knowing what the whole experience is for an animal from cradle (domestication) to grave (our bodies).

Though modern animal factories look nothing like what is idealized in children's books and advertisements, there are also many misconceptions about the practices and principles of a "humane" operation. The unappetizing process of turning live animals into isolated body parts and ground-up chunks of flesh begins at birth and ends in youth, as the animals are babies when they are sent to slaughter, whether they are raised conventionally or in operations that are labeled "humane," "sustainable," "natural," "free-range," "cage-free," "heritage-bred," "grass-fed" or "organic."

Whether it is a large or small enterprise, manipulating animals' reproductive systems for human gain is at the heart of the animal agriculture industry. The keeping of male studs, the stimulation of the genitals, the collection of semen, the castrating of males,

Slaughterhouse Statistics

- Number of animals killed per hour in the U.S.

660,000

- Occupation with the highest turnover rate in the U.S.

Slaughterhouse worker

- Occupation with the highest rate of on-the-job-injury in the U.S.

Slaughterhouse worker

Taken from: John Robbins, *Diet for a New America*, 1998.

and the insemination into the female are not exactly on people's minds when they sit down to dine. Many animals endure the stressful, often painful, and humiliating process of artificial insemination. Dairy cows are strapped into what the industry terms a "rape rack"; "natural turkeys" have to be artificially inseminated because their breasts are so large they're unable to mate in the usual manner; and "free-range" egg farms perpetuate unthinkable cruelty by buying their hens from egg hatcheries that kill millions of day-old male chicks every year.

Killing Is Not Humane

Many who speak of "humane" meat are really referring to the conditions under which animals are raised—not killed. And there's a big difference. When their bodies are fat enough for the dinner table, spent and overused from producing eggs and milk, and no longer useful in the way they were meant to be, as in the case of male studs on dairy farms, animals from both conventional and "humane" farms are all transported (first to the feedlot in the case of "beef cattle") to the slaughterhouse. The transportation process is excruciating and often fatal. The only law designed to "protect" animals in transport does not pertain to 95% of the animals killed for human consumption, as birds and rabbits (all classified as "poultry") are not protected. As a result, in transport, animals are forced to endure oppressive heat, bitter cold, stress, overcrowding, and respiratory problems from ammonia-laden urine.

Regardless of how they're raised, all animals killed for the refrigerated aisles of the grocery store are sent to mechanized slaughterhouses where their lives are brutally ended. By law, animals must be slaughtered at USDA-certified [U.S. Department of Agriculture] facilities, where horrific acts of cruelty occur on a daily basis. Everyone from federal meat inspectors to slaughterhouse workers have admitted to routinely witnessing the strangling, beating, scalding, skinning, and butchering of live, fully conscious animals. At small farms, where the owners can kill the animals themselves (in the case of birds) every one of them will

All animals that go into USDA-approved products must be slaughtered at a facility certified by the USDA, regardless of where the animals were raised.

tell you that, though it was hard in the beginning to slit the throat of the animals, it gets easier after awhile. I don't believe anyone would agree that it's healthy to detach and compartmentalize our emotions and become desensitized to violence and suffering. Compassionate people all have the same goal: the elimination of oppression, exploitation, and violence. Abuse, violence, cruelty—they all spring from the same source, and they all have the same effect—more abuse, more violence, more cruelty. The link between cruelty to animals and violence toward people has been well established.

When we tell ourselves we're eating meat from "humanely raised animals," we're leaving out a huge part of the equation.

There Is No Such Thing as Guilt-Free Meat   37

The slaughtering of an animal is a bloody and violent act, and death does not come easy for those who want to live.

Using Animal Products Creates Suffering

As much as we don't want to believe we are the cause of someone else's suffering, our consumption of meat, dairy, eggs and other animal products perpetuates the pointless violence and unnecessary cruelty that is inherent in the deliberate breeding and killing of animals for human consumption. If we didn't have a problem with it, we wouldn't have to make up so many excuses and justifications. We dance around the truth, label our choices "humane," and try to find some kind of compromise so we can have our meat and eat it, too.

The fundamental problems we keep running into do not arise merely from how we raise animals but that we eat animals. Clearly we can survive—and in fact, thrive—on a plant-based diet; we don't need to kill animals to be healthy, and in fact animal fat and protein are linked with many human diseases. What does it say about us that when given the opportunity to prevent cruelty and violence, we choose to turn away—because of tradition, culture, habit, convenience or pleasure? We are not finding the answers we are looking for because we are asking the wrong questions.

The movement toward "humanely raised food animals" simply assuages our guilt more than it actually reduces animal suffering. If we truly want our actions to reflect the compassion for animals we say we have, then the answer is very simple. We can stop eating them. How can this possibly be considered anything but a rational and merciful response to a violent and vacuous ritual? Every animal born into this world for his or her flesh, eggs or milk—only to be killed for human pleasure—has the same desire for maternal comfort and protection, the same ability to feel pain, and the same impulse to live as any living creature. There's nothing humane about breeding animals only to kill them, and there's nothing humane about ending the life of a healthy animal in his or her youth. In short, there is nothing humane about eating meat.

SIX

Technology Can Solve the Ethical Problems of Eating Meat

William Saletan

> "Every society lives with two kinds of moral problems: the ones it's ready to face, and the ones that will become clear or compelling only in retrospect," writes William Saletan in the following article. Perhaps one day, he suggests, we will look back on the way we kill and eat meat in the same way that we view such now-discarded customs as animal sacrifice and slavery. Still, he argues, humans like to eat meat. Saletan writes that the solution lies in technology, by growing meat in a process similar to the way tissue is grown from stems cells. Saletan writes about science and technology for the online magazine *Slate*.

Where were you when Barbaro broke his leg? [The Kentucky Derby champion broke his leg in the 2006 Preakness horse race.] I was at a steakhouse, watching the race on a big screen. I saw a horse pulling up, a jockey clutching him, a woman weeping. Thus began a worldwide vigil over the fate of the great horse. Would he be euthanized? Could doctors save him? In the restaurant, people watched and wondered. Then we went back to eating our steaks.

Shrinks call this "cognitive dissonance [the uncomfortable tension that comes from holding two conflicting thoughts at the same time]." You munch a strip of bacon then pet your dog. You wince at the sight of a crippled horse but continue chewing your burger. Three weeks ago, I took my kids to a sheep and wool festival. They petted lambs; I nibbled a lamb sausage. That's the thing about humans: We're half-evolved beasts. We love animals, but we love meat, too. We don't want to have to choose. And maybe we don't have to. Maybe, thanks to biotechnology, we can now grow meat instead of butchering it.

Eating Meat Might Be Outdated

With all the problems facing humanity—war, terrorism, poverty, tyranny—you probably don't worry much about whether it's right or wrong to eat meat. That's understandable. Every society lives with two kinds of moral problems: the ones it's ready to face, and the ones that will become clear or compelling only in retrospect. Human sacrifice, slavery, the subjugation of women—every tradition seems normal and indispensable until we're ready, morally and economically, to move beyond it.

The case for eating meat is like the case for other traditions: It's natural, it's necessary, and there's nothing wrong with it. But sometimes, we're mistaken. We used to think we were the only creatures that could manipulate grammar, make sophisticated plans, or recognize names out of context. In 2006 we've discovered the same skills in birds and dolphins. In recent years, we've learned that crows fashion leaves and metal into tools. Pigeons deceive each other. Rats run mazes in their dreams. Dolphins teach their young to use sponges as protection. Chimps can pick locks. Parrots can work with numbers. Dogs can learn words from context. We thought animals weren't smart enough to deserve protection. It turns out we weren't smart enough to realize they do.

Is meat-eating necessary? It was, back when our ancestors had no idea where their next meal might come from. Meat kept us alive and made us stronger. Many scientists think it played a crucial role in the development of the human brain. Now it's time to return the favor. Thousands of years ago, the human brain invented agriculture, and hunting lost its urgency. In the past two centuries, we've identified the nutrients in various kinds of meat, and we've learned how to get them instead from soy, nuts, and other vegetable sources. Meat has made us smart enough to figure out how we can live without it.

Humans Like to Eat Meat

So, why do we keep eating it? Because it's so darned tasty. Don't give me that hippie shtick about how McDonald's or Western society foisted beef on us. McDonald's didn't invent the appendix. McDonald's didn't invent all the genes we've acquired—at least eight, according to a 2004 article in the *Quarterly Review of*

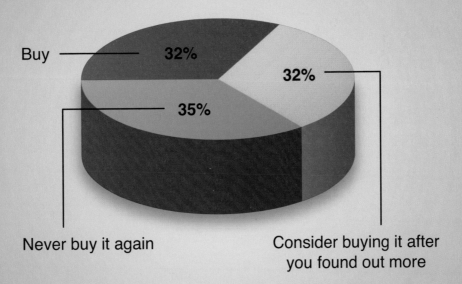

Question: Would You Buy Cloned Meat?

If the FDA determines that meat from cloned animals and their offspring is safe, and you learned that a food product you regularly purchase included meat from the offspring of cloned animals, would you . . .

Buy — 32%

32%

35%

Never buy it again

Consider buying it after you found out more

[Editor's note: In January 2008 the FDA announced that food cloned from livestock is safe to eat.]

Taken from: Maureen L. Storey, PhD, "Consumers' Knowledge, Attitudes, Beliefs, and Purchase Intent Regarding Foods from the Offspring of Cloned Animals," Center for Food, Nutrition, and Agriculture Policy, University of Maryland, December 14, 2006.

Biology—that help us, but not chimps, manage a meat diet. Look at the fossil evidence recently published in *Nature*. About 5,000 years ago, when people in Britain figured out how to domesticate cattle, sheep, and pigs, they promptly switched from fish-eating to meat-eating. A similar revolution swept North America about 700 years ago. My daughter has been demanding meat ever since she tasted it in baby food. I've seen vegetarian friends lust at the thought of a burger. We're carnivores. We evolved that way.

If we were just beasts, that would end the discussion. But we're not. Evolution didn't stop with our lusts; it started there. Food gave us brain power. Technology lifted us above survival and gave us time to think. We began to understand the operation of living things, even ourselves. We saw what we were, and we saw what we could be. That's the paradox of humanity: Our aspirations transcend our nature, but they have to respect it. To become what we must become, we have to work with what we are.

Technology may enable humans to grow meat tissue in a culture similar to the cultures used for growing stem cells.

Anyone familiar with Alcoholics Anonymous understands this duality. It's the heart of the Serenity Prayer: "God grant me the serenity to accept the things I cannot change, courage to change the things I can, and wisdom to know the difference." Many alcoholics take this to mean that addiction can't be changed, but behavior can, with God's help. But prayers often mean more than we understand. In the case of meat, maybe we don't have to go cold no-turkey. Maybe what we're asking for, what God is giving us, is the wisdom to see that we can't change our craving for meat, but we can change the way we satisfy it.

Technology Offers a Solution

How? By growing meat in labs, the way we grow tissue from stem cells. That's the great thing about cells: They're programmed to multiply. You just have to figure out what chemical and structural environment they need to do their thing. Researchers in Holland and the United States are working on the problem. They've grown and sautéed fish that smelled like dinner, though FDA rules didn't allow them to taste it. Now they're working on pork. The short-term goal is sausage, ground beef, and chicken nuggets. Steaks will be more difficult. Three Dutch universities and a nonprofit consortium called New Harvest are involved. They need money. A fraction of what we spend on cattle subsidies would help.

Growing meat like this will be good for us in lots of ways. We'll be able to make beef with no fat, or with good fat transplanted from fish. We'll avoid bird flu, mad-cow disease, and salmonella. We'll scale back the land consumption and pollution involved in cattle farming. But 300 years from now, when our descendants look back at slaughterhouses the way we look back at slavery, they won't remember the benefits to us, any more than they'll remember our dried-up tears for a horse. They'll want to know whether we saw the moral calling of our age. If we do, it's time to pony up.

SEVEN

Meat-Eating Causes Global Warming

Kathy Freston

Reducing car-exhaust emissions has been the focus of most proposals to fight global warming, but in the following essay Kathy Freston argues that our efforts would be better spent adopting a vegetarian diet. She cites a University of Chicago study that found that the land used to farm meat, plus the fossil fuels burned to transport it, make one calorie of meat protein ten times more environmentally costly than one calorie of plant protein. She also cites a meat-based diet's heavy use of water, production of harmful methane gas, and contribution to rain forest destruction. She points out that while switching to an environmentally friendly car is not something everyone can do, making the switch to a vegetarian diet is relatively easy. Freston is a self-health author and personal growth counselor.

President Herbert Hoover promised "a chicken in every pot and a car in every garage." With warnings about global warming reaching feverish levels, many are having second thoughts about all those cars. It seems they should instead be worrying about the chickens.

Kathy Freston, "Vegetarian Is the New Prius," Huffington Post, January 18, 2007. Reproduced by permission of huffingtonpost.com and Kathy Freston.

[In December 2006], the United Nations published a report on livestock and the environment with a stunning conclusion. "The livestock sector emerges as one of the top two or three most significant contributors to the most serious environmental problems, at every scale from local to global." It turns out that raising animals for food is a primary cause of land degradation, air pollution, water shortage, water pollution, loss of biodiversity and not least of all, global warming.

That's right, global warming. You've probably heard the story: emissions of greenhouse gases like carbon dioxide are changing our climate, and scientists warn of more extreme weather, coastal flooding, spreading disease, and mass extinctions. It seems that when you step outside and wonder what happened to winter, you might want to think about what you had for dinner last night. The UN report says almost a fifth of global warming emissions come from livestock (i.e., those chickens Hoover was talking about, plus pigs, cattle, and others)—that's more emissions than from all of the world's transportation combined. For a decade now, the image of Leonardo DiCaprio cruising in his hybrid Toyota Prius has defined the gold standard for environmentalism. These gas-sipping vehicles became a veritable symbol of the consumers' power to strike a blow against global warming. Just think: a car that could cut your vehicle emissions in half—in a country responsible for 25% of the world's total greenhouse gas emissions. Federal fuel economy standards languished in Congress, and average vehicle mileage dropped to its lowest level in decades, but the Prius showed people that another way is possible. Toyota could not import the cars fast enough to meet demand.

The Connection Between Meat and Fossil Fuels

[In 2006] researchers at the University of Chicago took the Prius down a peg when they turned their attention to another gas guzzling consumer purchase. They noted that feeding animals for meat, dairy, and egg production requires growing some ten times as much crops as we'd need if we just ate pasta primavera, faux chicken nuggets, and other plant foods. On top of that, we have to transport the

Some claim that greenhouse gases could be significantly reduced if enough people adopted a vegetarian diet, removing the need for methane-producing animals and the burning of fossil fuels to transport and process them.

animals to slaughterhouses, slaughter them, refrigerate their carcasses, and distribute their flesh all across the country. Producing a calorie of meat protein means burning more than ten times as much fossil fuels—and spewing more than ten times as much heat-trapping carbon dioxide—as does a calorie of plant protein. The researchers found that, when it's all added up, the average American does more to reduce global warming emissions by going vegetarian than by switching to a Prius.

According to the UN report, it gets even worse when we include the vast quantities of land needed to give us our steak and pork chops. Animal agriculture takes up an incredible 70% of all agricultural land, and 30% of the total land surface of the planet. As a result, farmed animals are probably the biggest cause of slashing and burning the world's forests. Today, 70% of former Amazon rainforest is used for pastureland, and feed crops cover much of the remainder. These forests serve as "sinks," absorbing carbon dioxide from the air, and burning these forests releases all the stored carbon dioxide, quantities that exceed by far the fossil fuel emission of animal agriculture.

As if that wasn't bad enough, the real kicker comes when looking at gases besides carbon dioxide—gases like methane and nitrous oxide, enormously effective greenhouse gases with 23 and 296 times the warming power of carbon dioxide, respectively. If carbon dioxide is responsible for about one-half of human-related greenhouse gas warming since the industrial revolution, methane and nitrous oxide are responsible for another one-third. These super-strong gases come primarily from farmed animals' digestive processes, and from their manure. In fact, while animal agriculture accounts for 9% of our carbon dioxide emissions, it emits 37% of our methane, and a whopping 65% of our nitrous oxide.

It's a little hard to take in when thinking of a small chick hatching from her fragile egg. How can an animal, so seemingly insignificant against the vastness of the earth, give off so much greenhouse gas as to change the global climate? The answer is in their sheer numbers. The United States alone slaughters more than 10 billion land animals every year, all to sustain a meat-ravenous culture that can barely conceive of a time not long ago when "a chicken in every pot" was considered a luxury. Land animals raised for food make up a staggering 20% of the entire land animal biomass of the earth. We are eating our planet to death.

What we're seeing is just the beginning, too. Meat consumption has increased five-fold in the past fifty years, and is expected to double again in the next fifty.

A Vegetarian Diet Is a Powerful Weapon Against Global Warming

It sounds like a lot of bad news, but in fact it's quite the opposite. It means we have a powerful new weapon to use in addressing the most serious environmental crisis ever to face humanity. The Prius was an important step forward, but how often are people in

The Food Diaries of Two Vegetarian Teens

Joey Galina, Lacto-Ovo Vegetarian, Age 14

"I love being a veggie because vegetarian food is always healthy, easy to make, and almost always tastes great!"

Breakfast:
Cereal ("Total") with soymilk and a banana, with calcium-fortified orange juice to drink
Snack:
Granola bar
Lunch:
Eggplant Rounds (a recipe from *The Teen's Vegetarian Cookbook* by Judy Krizmanic) with spaghetti, and I also had an orange. To drink: water
Snack:
Grapes and some unsalted peanuts
Dinner:
Stir-fry with brown rice, veggies, and tofu

Tabitha Nunes, Vegan, Age 16

"I enjoy being vegan so much I can't imagine living any other way."

Breakfast:
Apple cinnamon granola with vanilla soymilk
(Lots of water)
Lunch:
Vegan garden burger on toasted pita bread with broccoli sprouts, long grain brown rice, red peppers, and lettuce
(More water . . .)
Dinner:
Veggie stir-fry (cooked with soy margarine) with tofu on brown rice
Snack:
Garden of Eatin' blue corn chips

the market for a new car? Now that we know a greener diet is even more effective than a greener car, we can make a difference at every single meal, simply by leaving the animals off of our plates. Who would have thought: what's good for our health is also good for the health of the planet!

Going veg provides more bang for your buck than driving a Prius. Plus, that bang comes a lot faster. The Prius cuts emissions of carbon dioxide which spreads its warming effect slowly over a century. A big chunk of the problem with farmed animals, on the other hand, is methane, a gas which cycles out of the atmosphere in just a decade. That means less meat consumption quickly translates into a cooler planet. Not just a cooler planet, also a cleaner one. Animal agriculture accounts for most of the water consumed in this country, emits two-thirds of the world's acid-rain-causing ammonia, and is the world's largest source of water pollution— killing entire river and marine ecosystems, destroying coral reefs, and of course, making people sick. Try to imagine the prodigious volumes of manure churned out by modern American farms: 5 million tons a day, more than a hundred times that of the human population, and far more than our land can possibly absorb. The acres and acres of cesspools stretching over much of our countryside, polluting the air and contaminating our water, make the Exxon Valdez oil spill look minor in comparison. All of which we can fix surprisingly easily, just by putting down our chicken wings and reaching for a veggie burger.

Doing so has never been easier. Recent years have seen an explosion of environmentally-friendly vegetarian foods. Even chains like Ruby Tuesday, Johnny Rockets, and Burger King offer delicious veggie burgers and supermarket refrigerators are lined with heart-healthy creamy soymilk and tasty veggie deli slices. Vegetarian foods have become staples at environmental gatherings, and garnered celebrity advocates like Bill Maher, Alec Baldwin, Paul McCartney, and of course Leonardo DiCaprio. Just as the Prius showed us that we each have in our hands the power to make a difference against a problem that endangers the future of humanity, going vegetarian gives us a new way to dramatically reduce our dangerous emissions that is even more effective, easier to do, more accessible to everyone and certainly goes better with french fries.

EIGHT

A Vegan Diet Is the Best Way to Help the Planet

Bruce Friedrich

In the following essay, animal rights and environmental activist Bruce Friedrich argues that a vegan diet is the only reasonable diet for people who care about the environment. He writes that eating meat wastes and pollutes water, destroys rain forests, and wastes resources. He also cites studies showing that meat-eating is the number one cause of global warming. Considering the health benefits of a vegetarian diet, he writes, "There's no need or excuse to eat chickens, pigs, eggs and other animal products." Friedrich is the vice president for campaigns at People for the Ethical Treatment of Animals (PETA).

In 1987, I read *Diet for a Small Planet* by Frances Moore Lappé and—primarily for human rights and environmental reasons—went vegan. Two decades later, I still believe that—even leaving aside all the animal welfare issues—a vegan diet is the only reasonable diet for people in the developed world who care about the environment or global poverty.

Over the past 20 years, the environmental argument against growing crops to be fed to animals—so that humans can eat the animals—has grown substantially. Just this past November [2006], the environmental problems associated with eating chickens, pigs,

Bruce Friedrich, "Nuggets and Hummers and Fish Sticks, Oh My!" *Grist*, September 18, 2007. Reproduced by permission.

and other animals were the subject of a 408-page United Nations scientific report titled *Livestock's Long Shadow.*

The U.N. report found that the meat industry contributes to "problems of land degradation, climate change and air pollution, water shortage and water pollution, and loss of biodiversity." The report concludes that the meat industry is "one of the . . . most significant contributors to the most serious environmental problems, at every scale from local to global."

Eating Meat Is the No. 1 Consumer Cause of Global Warming

Al Gore, Leonardo DiCaprio, and others have brought the possibility of global cataclysm into sharp relief. What they have not been talking about, however, is the fact that all cars, trucks, planes, and other types of transportation *combined* account for about 13 percent of global warming emissions, whereas raising chickens, pigs, cattle, and other animals contributes to 18 percent, according to U.N. scientists. Yes, eating animal products contributes to global warming 40 percent more than all SUVs, 18-wheelers, jumbo jets, and other types of travel combined.

Al and Leo might not be talking about the connection between meat and global warming, but the Live Earth concert that Al inspired is: The recently published *Live Earth Global Warming Survival Handbook* recommends, "Don't be a chicken. Stop being a pig. And don't have a cow. Be the first on your block to cut back on meat." The *Handbook* further explains that "refusing meat" is "the *single most effective* thing you can do to reduce your carbon footprint" [emphasis in original].

And Environmental Defense, on its website, notes, "If every American skipped one meal of chicken per week and substituted vegetables and grains . . . the carbon dioxide savings would be the same as taking more than half a million cars off of U.S. roads." Imagine if we stopped eating animal products altogether.

Eating Meat Wastes Resources

If I lie in bed and never get up, I will burn almost 2,500 calories each day; that is what's required to keep my body alive. The same physiological reality applies to all animals: The vast majority of the calories consumed by a chicken, a pig, a cow, or another animal goes into keeping that animal alive, and once you add to that the calories required to create the parts of the animal that we don't eat (e.g., bones, feathers, and blood), you find that it takes more than 10 times as many calories of feed given to an animal to get one calorie back in the form of edible fat or muscle. In other words, it's exponentially more efficient to eat grains, soy, or oats directly rather than feed them to farmed animals so that humans can eat those animals. It's like tossing more than 10 plates of spaghetti into the trash for every one plate you eat.

And that's just the pure "calories in, calories out" equation. When you factor in everything else, the situation gets much worse. Think about the extra stages of production that are required to get dead chickens, pigs, or other animals from the farm to the table:

1. Grow more than 10 times as much corn, grain, and soy (with all the required tilling, irrigation, crop dusters, and so on), as would be required if we ate the plants directly.
2. Transport—in gas-guzzling, pollution-spewing 18-wheelers—all that grain and soy to feed manufacturers.
3. Operate the feed mill (again, using massive amounts of resources).
4. Truck the feed to the factory farms.
5. Operate the factory farms.
6. Truck the animals many miles to slaughterhouses.
7. Operate the slaughterhouses.
8. Truck the meat to processing plants.
9. Operate the meat processing plants.
10. Truck the meat to grocery stores (in refrigerated trucks).
11. Keep the meat in refrigerators or freezers at the stores.

With every stage comes massive amounts of extra energy usage—and with that comes heavy pollution and massive amounts of greenhouse gases, of course. Obviously, vegan foods require some of these stages, too, but vegan foods cut out the factory farms, the slaughterhouses, and multiple stages of heavily polluting tractor-trailer trucks, as well as all the resources (and pollution) involved in each of those stages. And as was already

It has been suggested that growing animals for food is an inefficient use of resources, as it requires massive amounts of energy and contributes to soil, water, and air pollution.

noted, vegan foods require less than one-tenth as many calories from crops, since they are turned directly into food rather than funneled through animals first.

Eating Meat Wastes and Pollutes Water

All food requires water, but animal foods are exponentially more wasteful of water than vegan foods are. Enormous quantities of water are used to irrigate the corn, soy, and oat fields that are dedicated to feeding farmed animals—and massive amounts of water are used in factory farms and slaughterhouses. According to the National Audubon Society, raising animals for food requires about as much water as *all other water uses combined*. Environmental author John Robbins estimates that it takes about 300 gallons of water to feed a vegan for a day, four times as much water to feed [a lacto-ovo] vegetarian, and about *14 times as much* water to feed a meat-eater.

Raising animals for food is also a water-polluting process. According to a report prepared by U.S. Senate researchers, animals raised for food in the U.S. produce 86,000 pounds of excrement per second—that's 130 *times* more than the amount of excrement that the entire human population of the U.S. produces! Farmed animals' excrement is more concentrated than human excrement, and is often contaminated with herbicides, pesticides, toxic chemicals, hormones, antibiotics, and other harmful substances. According to the Environmental Protection Agency, the runoff from factory farms pollutes our rivers and lakes *more than all other industrial sources combined*.

Eating Meat Destroys the Rain Forest

The World Bank recently reported that *90 percent of all Amazon rain forest land cleared since 1970 is used for meat production*. It's not just that we're destroying the rain forest to make grazing land for cows—we're also destroying it to grow feed for them and other animals. Last year, Greenpeace targeted KFC for the destruction of rain forests because the Amazon is being razed to grow feed for chickens that end up in KFC's buckets. Of course, the rain forest is being used to grow feed for other chickens, pigs, and cows, too (i.e., KFC isn't the only culprit).

What About Eating Fish?

Anyone who reads the news knows that commercial fishing fleets are plundering the oceans and destroying sensitive aquatic ecosystems at an incomprehensible rate. One super-trawler is the length of a football field, and can take in 800,000 pounds of fish in a single netting. These trawlers scrape along the ocean floor, clear-cutting coral reefs and everything else in their path. Hydraulic dredges scoop up huge chunks of the ocean floor to sift out scallops, clams, and oysters. Most of what the fishing fleets pull in isn't even eaten by human beings; half is fed to animals raised for food, and about 30 million tons each year are just tossed back into the ocean, dead, with disastrous and irreversible consequences for the natural biological balance.

Then there is aquaculture (fish farming), which is increasing at a rate of more than 10 percent annually. Aquaculture is even

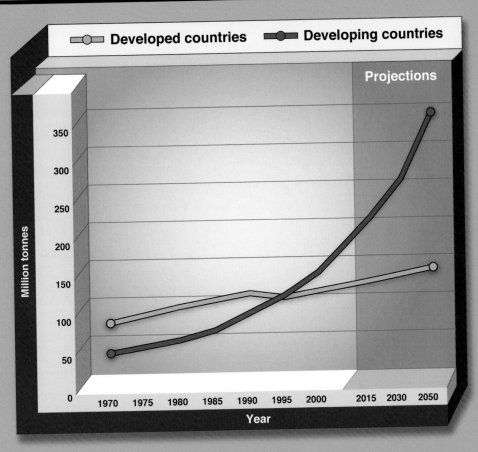

Past and Projected Meat Production in Developed and Developing Countries from 1970 to 2050

Taken from: Food and Agriculture Organization of the United Nations, 2006.

worse than commercial fishing because, for starters, it takes about four pounds of wild-caught fish to reap just one pound of farmed fish, which eat fish caught by commercial trawlers. Farmed fish are often raised in the same water that wild fish swim in, but fish farmers dump antibiotics into the water and use genetic breeding to create "Frankenstein fish." The antibiotics contaminate the oceans and seas, and the genetically engineered fish sometimes escape and breed with wild fish, throwing delicate aquatic balances off-kilter. Researchers at the University of Stockholm demonstrated that the horrible environmental impact of fish farms can extend to an area 50,000 times larger than the farm itself.

Eating Meat Supports Cruelty

Caring for the environment means protecting all of our planet's inhabitants, not just the human ones. Chickens, pigs, turkeys, fish, and cows are intelligent, social animals who feel pain, just as humans, dogs, and cats do. Chickens and pigs do better on animal behavior cognition tests than dogs or cats, and are interesting individuals in the same way. Fish form strong social bonds, and some even use tools. Yet these animals suffer extreme pain and deprivation in today's factory farms. Chickens have their sensitive beaks cut off with a hot blade, pigs have their tails chopped off and their teeth removed with pliers, and cattle and pigs are castrated—all without any pain relief. The animals are crowded together and given steady doses of hormones and antibiotics in order to make them grow so quickly that their hearts and limbs often cannot keep up, causing crippling and heart attacks. At the slaughterhouse, they are hung upside-down and bled to death, often while they are still conscious.

What About Eating Meat That Is Not from Factory-Farmed Animals?

Is meat better if it doesn't come from factory-farmed animals? Of course, but its production still wastes resources and pollutes the environment. Shouldn't we environmentalists challenge ourselves to do the best we can, not just to make choices that are a bit less bad?

The U.N. report looks at meat at a global level and indicts the inefficiency and waste that are inherent in meat production. No matter where meat comes from, raising animals for food will require that exponentially more calories be fed to animals than they can produce in their flesh, and it will require all those extra stages of CO_2-intensive production as well. Only grass-fed cows eat food from land that could not otherwise be used to grow food for human beings, and even grass-fed cows require much more water and create much more pollution than vegan foods do.

The case against eating animal products is ironclad; it's not a new argument, and it goes way beyond just global warming. Animals will not grow or produce flesh, milk, or eggs without food and water; they won't do it without producing excrement; and the stages of meat, dairy, and egg production will always cause pollution and be resource-intensive.

If the past is any guide, this essay will generate much hand-wringing from my meat-eating environmentalist colleagues and, sadly, some anger. They will prefer half-measures (e.g., meat that is "not as bad" as other meat). They may accuse PETA of being judgmental—simply for presenting the evidence. They will make various arguments that are beside the point. They will ignore the overwhelming argument against eating animal products and try to find a loophole. Some will just call the argument absurd, presenting no evidence at all.

But as Leonardo DiCaprio has noted, this is the 11th hour for the environment. Where something as basic as eating animals is concerned, the choice could not be any clearer. Every time we sit down to eat, we can choose to eat a product that is, according to U.N. scientists, "one of the . . . most significant contributors to the most serious environmental problems, at every scale from local to global," or we can choose vegan—and preferably organic—foods. It's bad for the environment to eat animals. It's time to stop looking for loopholes.

Considering the proven health benefits of a vegetarian diet—the American Dietetic Association states that vegetarians have a reduced risk of obesity, heart disease, and various types of cancer—there's no need or excuse to eat chickens, pigs, eggs, and other animal products. And vegan foods are available everywhere and taste great; as with all foods—vegan or not—you just need to find the ones you like.

NINE

A Vegetarian Diet Is Not Always the Best Choice for the Environment

Brendan I. Koerner

In the following selection, environmental columnist Brendan I. Koerner weighs the environmental effects of vegan, vegetarian, and meat-based diets to discover which one is best for the planet. The answer: It depends. While a vegan diet produces fewer greenhouse gases, in some cases raising cattle livestock may be a more efficient use of land. Instead of trying to convert people to a vegetarian diet, Koerner argues, it would be wiser to try to get people to limit their meat consumption. Koerner writes The Green Lantern column for *Slate*.

As a longtime vegetarian, I've always been confident that my diet is better for the planet than that of your typical carnivore. But a vegan pal of mine says I could be doing a lot more, by rejecting all animal products—no eggs, no milk, not even the occasional bowl of mac 'n cheese. Is veganism really that much better for the environment?

Since few Americans have followed actress Alicia Silverstone's abstemious [sparing in consumption of] lead and renounced animal products altogether, there aren't many data available on the environmental consequences of veganism. Somewhere between 2 percent and 5 percent of the nation's eaters classify themselves as vegetarians; of that number, perhaps 5 percent are strict vegans. As a result, most research on meat-free diets has focused on lacto-ovo vegetarians, the milk-and-egg eaters who form the lion's share of the veggie demographic.

According to a 2005 University of Chicago study, a lacto-ovo vegetarian emits far less greenhouse gas than a counterpart adhering to the standard, meat-rich American diet—the difference is equivalent to around 1.5 metric tons of carbon dioxide per year, assuming the same daily caloric intake. (The study's authors thus claim that going vegetarian has the same effect on carbon dioxide emissions as switching from a Chevrolet Suburban to a Toyota Camry.) The savings mostly come about because of the disparity between the fossil fuel required to produce a calorie's worth of grain vs. that needed to make a calorie's worth of beef; grain is nearly a dozen times more efficient in this regard. Cattle are also a huge source of methane, a particularly noxious greenhouse gas; it's estimated that bovines are responsible for roughly triple the methane emissions of the American coal industry.

Yet lacto-ovo vegetarians still derive about 14 percent of their calories from animal products. Bring that number down to zero, as strict vegans do, and you'll certainly ratchet down your carbon emissions by another several hundred pounds per year. "If we put [greenhouse gas] emissions above all else, then veganism beats lacto-ovo vegetarianism handily," says Gidon Eshel, a co-author of the University of Chicago study. "That much is clear and unequivocal."

Carbon Dioxide Emissions Are Only Part of the Impact

But Eshel hastens to add—and The Lantern wholeheartedly agrees—that your vegan acquaintance isn't necessarily some environmental saint. That's because direct carbon dioxide emissions are only part of the story when it comes to food's eco-impact. You also have to look at the issue of land use—specifically how much and what sort of land is required to sustain an agricultural enterprise. In a region with poor-to-mediocre soil, for example, it

In some cases, land that may not support planting of crops, like wheat, may be suitable for growing of animals for food.

may be more efficient to operate a well-managed egg farm than to try growing vegetables that can't flourish under such conditions. And animals are handy at consuming low-quality grain that isn't necessarily fit for human consumption. (Rather than going to waste, that grain can help create nutrient-rich dairy products.) In fact, a recent Cornell University study concluded that modest carnivorousness may actually be better for the environment than outright vegetarianism, since cattle can graze on inferior land not suitable for crops. Squeezing more calories out of the land means that less food needs be imported from elsewhere, thereby reducing the burning of fossil fuels.

That's music to the ears of The Lantern, a devoted meat-eater who weeps at the very thought of life without bacon cheeseburgers and curry goat. But there are important caveats to the Cornell study: First, its calculations assume that all meat is raised locally, rather than frozen and trucked cross-country; second, the study recommended that to optimize land use, residents of New York state (where the research was conducted) limit their meat and egg consumption to two cooked ounces per day—3.8 ounces less than the national average.

It Is Unrealistic to Expect Everyone to Eat a Vegetarian Diet

Though The Lantern admires the ascetic fortitude of vegetarians and vegans, it's pretty unrealistic to expect the majority of adult Americans to forgo steak for the benefit of the planet. At the same

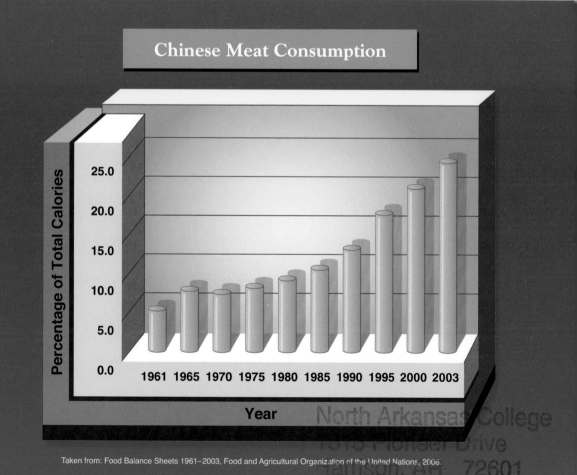

Taken from: Food Balance Sheets 1961–2003, Food and Agricultural Organization of the United Nations, 2006.

time, agriculture is responsible for between 17 percent and 20 percent of the nation's energy consumption. So instead of hectoring people to become vegetarians—a tactic that causes many Americans to roll their eyes—perhaps we should start by urging consumers to be more cognizant of exactly how much energy it takes to produce and transport an Extra-Long Bacon Cheddar Cheesesteak. And it wouldn't hurt if people got wise to the fact that meat needn't be the focus of every breakfast, lunch, and dinner.

That's going to be a serious challenge, however, considering that per capita meat consumption rose by 40 percent in the United States between 1961 and 2002. One hopes that the Chinese don't follow our gluttonous lead, but the news so far isn't encouraging: Meat consumption in China has already doubled over the past decade.

TEN

Sustainably Raised Meat Is a Healthy Alternative

Diane Hatz

> In the following selection, Diane Hatz argues that environmental and health problems associated with meat are not from the meat itself, but from factory farming and commercial slaughterhouses. She describes the problems of the current production system such as disease, unsafe working conditions, and overmedicated animals, and promotes sustainably farmed, grass-fed meat as the solution. Such a system, she writes, yields healthier meat and a healthier ecosystem as well. Hatz is the founder and director of Sustainable Table, an organization that educates consumers on issues surrounding the sustainable food and agriculture movement.

Beef has always been considered part of the All American meal, conjuring up images of cowboys riding horses under blue Western skies with cattle grazing on the wide open range. Hamburgers at 4th of July cookouts; roast on Sundays; and steak for special occasions are all part of many Americans' diets.

In the past several decades, though, eating beef has become less popular due to health concerns, including an increased risk of heart disease, high blood pressure and increased cholesterol levels. And, more recently, mad cow disease and other issues such as

Diane Hatz, "Beef," *Sustainable Table*, September 2005. www.sustainabletable.org. Reproduced by permission.

Commercial Red Meat Production in the United States

November 2007	
Type	**Million Pounds**
Beef	2,229.1
Veal	10.1
Pork	2,045.4
Lamb and mutton	16.1
Total red meat	4,300.7

Taken from: "Livestock Slaughter," National Agricultural Statistics Service, December 21, 2007.

artificial growth hormones and antibiotic-resistant bacteria have made consumers even more concerned.

The problem, though, is not with the beef. The problem is with the way beef is raised and our tendency to eat oversized portions of food. . . .

Beef Gets a Bad Rap

Beef has gotten a bad rap. Too much red meat can contribute to a variety of health problems, though it's not the meat that's necessarily the problem; it's the way the animal is raised (and how much of it you're eating!). Cattle used to be raised on pasture year round, from birth to slaughter, where they fed off the natural grasses and hay that grew on the land. Cows are ruminants and are by nature vegetarians.

In recent years, though, cattle production has become more centralized and most animals are now "finished" on feedlots. Finishing is the process of preparing animals for slaughter—the length of time an animal is finished depends on the practices of the farmer. The longer the finishing time, the higher the chance the animal is being raised on a factory farm.

Factory farm feedlots are usually large, confined areas where cattle are finished before slaughter. Massive amounts of feces and urine are accumulated in this confined area after the cattle are fed large amounts of grain and byproducts such as outdated human food, dairy products, chicken litter (which contains manure, feathers, bedding materials, and possibly scraps from dead animals), as well as other byproducts that are cheap and readily available. These types of feed additives are not healthy for the animal.

The practice of feeding cow parts back to cattle spreads mad cow disease, a highly infectious disease that kills a cow by destroying the animal's brain. The practice was banned in 1997, but several loopholes in the regulations leave open the possibility that cow remains could be fed back to cattle. (Cows are by nature vegetarian and should not be fed any type of animal product.) Over a hundred cases of the human form of mad cow disease have been documented and have been attributed to eating meat from infected animals.

All animals that are given feed additives should be avoided—in cattle, the most common additives are hormones that are implanted in the animals to make them grow faster and non-therapeutic antibiotics, which are fed to the animals in low doses to help ward off disease. There are a variety of health issues associated with these practices. . . .

More Problems with the Meat Industry

Another problem with today's meat supply is the meat inspection system and slaughterhouses. To increase profits, line speeds have been increased dramatically, to the point where workers in processing facilities are said to have one of the most dangerous jobs of all. Injuries are very common. The facilities are also unsanitary, making the meat more susceptible to such pathogens and bacteria like *E. coli* and salmonella. To make matters worse, the meat inspection system is now more focused on paperwork, instead of visually inspecting meat.

Instead of trying to solve the problems plaguing the meat industry, food irradiation is being touted as the solution. Food irradiation is a process where high levels of radiation are shot through the meat to kill off bacteria. It is a controversial process that destroys the nutrient content of the food and creates new compounds that have not been tested for safety.

Farmers that practice sustainable methods of agriculture raise their cattle on pasture and either feed them grasses only, or supplement the grasses with controlled amounts of grain. By controlling the amount of grain fed to the animal, the meat will still have the marbled texture and flavor that most consumers are used to (meaning the meat will have the fat in it that gives it the taste we are used to), but the animal will not get sick from eating too much grain. A general guideline to remember is that the more grain fed to the animal, the more fat in the meat; and the more fat in the meat, the less healthy it is for you.

The Health Benefits of Grass-Fed Meat

Grass-fed, or pasture-raised meat, is the healthiest beef you can buy. Truly pasture-raised cattle spend their lives on pasture, eating only the grasses and hay that nature intended them to eat.

The health benefits include:
- Less total fat—Pasture-raised beef can have the same amount of fat as a skinless chicken breast.
- Less calories—A 6 ounce steak from a pasture-raised cow can have 100 fewer calories than a 6 ounce steak from a factory farmed animal.
- More Omega 3's—There are two to four times more of these "good" fats in pasture-raised beef.
- Higher amounts of Vitamin E—Vitamin E helps reduce the risk of heart disease and cancer.

Watch Serving Sizes

Anything in excess is unhealthy, so the quantity of meat eaten also determines how healthy it is for you. In the United States, the average adult male eats 154% of the recommended daily allowance (RDA) for protein (97 grams versus the recommended 63 grams), and the average adult female eats 127% of the RDA (63.5

In 2008 the Westland Meat Company recalled and disposed of contaminated meat that had been shipped to the Los Angeles Unified School District.

vs. 50 grams). [Sixty-seven percent] of that protein comes from consuming animal protein (as opposed to the rest of the world which averages 34%). And of the 273 pounds of meat the average American eats in a year, 97 pounds of that is from beef.

The average portion of meat that should be eaten in a day is two three-ounce servings (three ounces is roughly the size of a deck of cards). Active male teens and men can have up to seven ounces of meat daily. Consumers in industrialized societies, especially the United States, are eating much more meat than is healthy for them. So, not only do we need to look at the type of meat we're eating, we need to look at how much of it we're putting into our bodies. Read the US Department of Agriculture and Department of Health and Human Services' Dietary Guidelines for Americans 2005 for their suggestions on the type and quantity of foods that are healthiest for you.

The healthiest beef to eat is sustainably raised meat from animals raised on pasture. This can either be organic meat or sustainable.

Pasture-raised beef tastes different than fatty, factory farm meat. It has much less fat, which means it needs to be cooked differently.

The Hidden Costs of Industrially Raised Meat

Two reasons consumers buy a particular brand of meat are most often because of price and convenience. Consumers want to pay as little as possible for something they can easily find. Unfortunately, in this day and age, we can find items such as meat everywhere for a relatively low price.

The problem is that any type of industrially raised or factory farm meat that you buy is actually much more expensive than you realize, much more than what is on the price tag. These hidden costs are called externalities. A 2005 study published in the *International Journal of Agricultural Sustainability* estimated that these costs range from $5.7 billion to $16.9 billion a year in the United States.

In addition to eventual medical bills from heart disease and other illnesses brought on by eating too much saturated fat from meat, there are other costs that influence the true price of food. These costs include:

- Environmental pollution from factory farms
- Health threats such as antibiotic-resistant bacteria and food-borne pathogens
- Fossil fuels that are used to raise and transport animals and animal products
- Destruction of rural communities throughout the country
- Large payments (subsidies) that are given to industrial farms and come out of our tax dollars!

But the bottom line when you're standing at the cash register is how much the meat costs. Sustainably raised meat will always cost more than factory farmed meat—it has to because the animals are given better food and attention, and they are raised in better conditions, which costs more money. Smaller farms are also not given the large subsidies that larger farms receive. Currently, organic meat can cost two to three times more than factory farmed.

So what can you do? Eat less! Look at how much meat you eat each day and how much animal protein you are supposed to eat (no more than 6 or 7 ounces per day). If you cut your meat intake in half, you still might be over the recommended daily allowance. By cutting your intake in half, you can then spend more for sustainably raised meat. And when more people demand healthier, more humane meat, more will be raised, which will then lower the price you pay for it.

ELEVEN

Vegans Have to Constantly Defend Their Lifestyle

Gaia Veenis

> Becoming a vegan, writes Gaia Veenis in the following essay, was a satisfying decision and a natural outgrowth of her pacifist and feminist beliefs. What was surprisingly difficult about her new lifestyle was having to deal with other people who did not understand or support her choice. She writes of fielding questions about what she can eat and whether she is getting enough protein, and of people who view her as pretentious or her decision as a passing fancy. Veenis wrote this as a staff writer and journalism senior at San Diego State University.

About three months ago, I made a decision I couldn't feel better about. A vegetarian since age 10, I decided to become vegan, ridding my life of all animal products. I knew it would be difficult investigating the foods and products to use, but so far the most challenging aspect has been constantly defending my lifestyle.

Reactions vary when I tell people I'm vegan. Some people think there's nothing I can eat, or I won't get the protein I need. Others think my being a vegan is a pretentious phase or hobby. There are some people who respect my position, though they may not be interested in veganism themselves. Nevertheless, there are others who roll their eyes and sigh when I do nothing more than refuse to eat the foods they love.

The notion about a vegan's limited menu is false. I've been forced to be more creative and diversify my diet since making this decision. I cook at home more often, use more fresh vegetables and fruits and have started creating my own recipes even my carnivorous roommate enjoys. There are also many vegan-friendly restaurants in San Diego.

Vegans Get Enough Protein

The idea vegans can't get the sufficient protein is also untrue. I don't get protein the same ways average Americans do; however,

Restaurants devoting themselves to vegetarian cuisine help people to adopt vegetarianism as a lifestyle that persists beyond occasional trends.

increasing my intake of beans, nuts, soy products and protein-rich vegetables gives me the protein my body requires. I also get all the calcium found in a glass of cow's milk from a glass of soymilk.

Many people tell me they understand why I would be vegetarian; not wanting to eat dead animals is understandable and the disgusting practices of the meat industry are notorious. However, they often consider being vegan too extreme. But the cruelty animals endure in the meat industry is mirrored in the dairy and egg industries. Plus, many seemingly vegetarian foods contain gelatin, which is made of hooves. I could no longer ignore these facts as I did in my vegetarian years.

The average egg-laying hen lives her life in a cage with less than half a square foot of space, according to the National Animal Health

Teen Eating Habits in the United States, 2005

Dietary Habits of 8- to 18-Year-Olds

- 6 percent never eat meat.

- 6 percent never eat poultry.

- 24 percent never eat fish/seafood.

- 3 percent never eat dairy products.

- 8 percent never eat eggs.

- 22 percent never eat honey.

- 3 percent never eat meat, poultry, fish/seafood (vegetarian).

- 1 percent never eat meat, poultry, dairy products/eggs (vegan, except possibly honey).

Taken from: Charles Stahler, "How Many Youths Are Vegetarian?" *Vegetarian Journal*, Issue 4, 2005.

Monitoring System Web site. Hens are usually subjected to beak trimming to keep [them] from attacking each other under these stressful conditions. Chickens may be stupid, but they still feel pain and don't deserve to have their beaks cut off with searing blades.

The dairy industry also profits from oppressing animals. According to "Scientific Farm Animal Production," by Thomas G. Field, most dairy cows are killed after five or six years of giving milk. They are rarely allowed to nurse their young, who are often taken away after birth to be slaughtered or raised as "special-fed veal."

Veganism Is Not a Trend

The most bothersome false assumption is that veganism is a trend, and that I can give it up when my mood changes. I'd never tell someone who became religious that they were just following a trendy hobby. Furthermore, I don't look down on people who eat animal products, so there's no reason people should belittle my lifestyle.

Becoming vegan was a personal and moral decision, one that's been a natural progression of my feminist and pacifist beliefs. I've loved animals my entire life, and when I began speaking out against the oppression of women, children, minorities, and poor people, it led me to decide not to rely on using animals to feed and clothe myself. It's time people recognize why vegans live the way we do, so the next time I tell someone why I'm not eating cheese, they might understand.

TWELVE

A Flexitarian Diet Offers a Less Strict Option to Vegetarianism

Carolyn O'Neil

> In the following article, Carolyn O'Neil recommends a middle ground between a meat-eating diet and a vegetarian diet. The so-called flexitarian diet refers to an eating plan that is high in vegetable protein and vegetarian choices but allows for occasional meat consumption. Such a diet, O'Neil writes, has been endorsed by such mainstays of vegetarianism as People for the Ethical Treatment of Animals (PETA) and Mollie Katzen, author of the pioneering vegetarian cookbook *Moosewood Cookbook*. PETA's argument, she reports, is that two part-time vegetarians could make the same impact as one full-time vegetarian. And Katzen is herself now a flexitarian. O'Neil is a registered dietitian and coauthor of *The Dish on Eating Healthy and Being Fabulous!*

Have you ever wanted to become a vegetarian because you love vegetables and know a plant-based diet is really healthy but you just couldn't quite commit to banning burgers and pork chops from your life?

Well, you don't have to go cold turkey on turkey. An increasingly popular middle ground between vegetarian and meat eater is emerging, and it has a name: flexitarian.

Carolyn O'Neil, "'Flexitarian' Easier than Being Vegetarian," *Atlanta Journal-Constitution*, November 14, 2007. Republished with permission of the *Atlanta Journal-Constitution*, conveyed through Copyright Clearance Center, Inc.

Sometimes flexitarians eat vegetarian-style meals and sometimes they eat meat. It could mean whole-wheat penne pasta for lunch and short ribs for dinner. But often it's a smaller serving of meat with lots of side vegetables.

According to the Vegeterian Research Group, about 3 percent of American adults are true vegeterians who say they never eat meat, fish or poultry. But at least 10 percent of adults consider themselves vegetarians even though they eat fish or chicken occasionally. The flexitarian model, where people say they "seek out

Categories of Food Consumers

Vegans:

Do not eat meat, poultry, fish, dairy, eggs, or honey

Strict Vegetarians:

Do not eat meat, poultry, or fish

Flexitarians (include the groups below):

• **Vegetarian:**

Those who say they are vegetarian, or "almost vegetarian," but eat some meat, poultry, or fish

• **Vegetarian-inclined:**

Replace meat with meat alternatives for at least some meals; usually maintain a vegetarian diet or eat four or more meatless meals per week

• **Health conscious:**

Strive for a balanced eating plan or eat two or three meatless meals per week

Taken from: Vegetarian Resource Group. www.vrg.org.

vegetarian meals," fits even more folks; estimates are as high as 30 percent to 40 percent of the U.S. population.

The definition has even made it to Wikipedia. "Flexitarianism is a term used to describe the practice of eating mainly vegetarian food, but making occasional exceptions for social, pragmatic, cultural, or nutritional reasons. They may eat meat and/or other animal products sometimes."

For example, a flexitarian might cook vegetarian dishes at home but eat dishes including meat or fish at a restaurant or at a friend's house.

Flexitarian Fast Food?

Arguably, even fast-food joints are flexitarian if they offer a veggie burger, but many diners want more. The increased demand for vegetarian dishes has raised the bar so that simply offering a vegetable plate or grilled mushroom sandwich isn't enough.

At Repast Restaurant in Atlanta, chefs and co-owners Mihoko Obunai and Joseph Truex have flexed their organic and seasonal menus to adapt to the sometimes-I-feel-like-a-vegetarian trend by offering customers a selection of meats and seafood as well as Obunai's Japanese-style macrobiotic compositions.

Using the "f" word right upfront, Peter Berley, chef at Broadway East, a new restaurant in New York City, draws menu inspiration from his cookbook, *The Flexitarian Table: Inspired, Flexible Meals for Vegetarians, Meat Lovers and Everyone in Between.*

The recipes in the book, and the menu, offer mix-and-match convertible combinations that can be prepared with or without meats. There's a choice of either baked fish or ricotta dumplings served over French lentils. The Gratin of Cherry Tomatoes and White Beans can be served with or without sardines.

Even Small Changes Make a Difference

While eating more like a vegetarian doesn't automatically translate to a healthier diet (high-fat foods like broccoli smothered in cheese sauce and biscuits slathered with butter are vegetarian choices), nutrition research identifies a plant-based diet rich in

GO VEGAN
TO REDUCE
GLOBAL WARMING

ONE VEGAN SAVES
1.6 TONS
GREENHOUSE GASES
PER YEAR!

ANIMA
: PLAN

The adoption of a vegetarian diet, even on a small scale, can have a significant impact on one's health and on the environment.

whole grains, beans, nuts, fruits and vegetables as being the best at preventing disease and obesity.

And to reap health benefits, you don't have to go to tofu and bean sprouts full time. The USDA's My Pyramid diet guidelines encourage all healthy Americans to vary protein choices by substituting beans or peas as a main dish or part of a meal often.

And even the notoriously tough pundits at People for the Ethical Treatment of Animals support part-time vegetarianism, arguing that if two people cut their meat and fish intake in half, it has the same impact as one person going vegetarian.

But perhaps the most compelling reason to spend more mealtime with the vegetable kingdom is culinary. Mollie Katzen, famous for her iconic vegetarian "Moosewood Cookbook," published more than 20 years ago, is a self-professed flexitarian now, too.

Her best-selling new cookbook, "The Vegetable Dishes I Can't Live Without," was written to appeal to food lovers who like their vegetables with meat or without.

Meatless Menu Options

Here are choices to add protein without meat:

Choose beans or peas as a main dish or part of a meal often. Some choices are:

- Chili with kidney or pinto beans
- Stir-fried tofu
- Split pea, lentil, minestrone or white bean soups
- Baked beans
- Black bean enchiladas
- Garbanzo or kidney beans on a chef's salad
- Rice and beans
- Veggie burgers or garden burgers
- Hummus (chickpeas) spread on pita bread

Choose nuts as a snack, on salads, or in main dishes. Some ideas:

- Use pine nuts in pesto sauce for pasta.
- Add slivered almonds to steamed vegetables.
- Add toasted peanuts or cashews to a vegetable stir-fry instead of meat
- Sprinkle a few nuts on top of low-fat ice cream or frozen yogurt
- Add walnuts or pecans to a green salad instead of cheese or meat

THIRTEEN

Raw Foods Are the Answer

Bob McCauley

In the following selection, Bob McCauley promotes the benefits of a raw food diet. According to McCauley, cooking foods makes them more difficult to digest and destroys crucial enzymes that the body needs to absorb nutrients. "When you cook food," he writes, "you tame it, de-claw it, rob it of savage vitality as well as its ability to renew and cleanse the body at a cellular level." He cites cooked and highly processed foods as key in breaking down the immune system and creating chronic health conditions such as dementia and cancer. McCauley is a writer on health and founder of the Watershed Wellness Center, a health products company.

We are designed to live 120–150 years, yet making it to 100 without the onset of senility is next to impossible. Your chances of contracting Alzheimer's or some dementia-related disease by age 85 is now 50/50. This occurs because of toxin accumulation in the body, particularly the brain, which it is prone to because of its very texture and material it is composed of. It is also the most difficult place to hydrate in the body. Toxins accumulate after a lifetime of eating cooked foods and not drinking enough water. Over the years, denatured (cooked) foods deposit

Bob McCauley, "Raw Foods Rule," *Watershed Wellness*, 2007. Reproduced by permission.

acid waste and a plethora of other toxins throughout the body, especially accumulating in the joints, in and around the organs and in the brain. Dementia-related diseases are a sure sign of a lifetime of chronic dehydration. Every time you take a sip of water, 80% of it is used by the brain, especially to supply the cranial fluids. When we fail to do this over a lifetime, toxins begin to interfere with the brain's delicate chemical balance. Once a single chemical reaction in the brain is stopped or significantly altered, the ripple effect will be felt throughout the brain. How it will manifest itself exactly will depend on the person's background, diet, etc.

Raw fruits and vegetables contain enzymes and nutritional chemicals that aid digestion and enhance the immune system, but they are lost during the cooking process.

Reversing these psychiatric conditions is not easy, but can be done to some degree by following the *Raw Food Rules* and drinking 2–3 gallons of *Ionized Water* each day. I drink 2 gallons myself everyday and it not hard to do at all.

All foods contain certain levels of natural toxins in them such as heavy metals. For instance, *Chlorella* [a green algae used by some as food source] contains lead as well as other toxins, however they are minute and will not deposit in the body because it is fresh, i.e. raw, NOT denatured by cooking, pasteurizing or other forms of processing. Examine any food, organic or commercially grown, and you will find toxins that deposit in the body in dangerous levels *only* when it is consumed after it is cooked or otherwise denatured.

I would like to point out that it is difficult to get *Chlorella* manufacturers to admit these toxins exist in their products, however there are a few who openly speak of it. However, these toxins will be removed when the food is consumed raw. *Chlorella* is famous for removing heavy metals such as lead, which is why toxins consumed with raw vegetables are not deposited in the body.

Chronic disease doesn't exist in the wild. Animals don't have the long life span that we could have if we wanted. But there are other things to consider with animals in the wild.

Raw Foods Are More Nutritious

When you eat raw foods, you know you are really eating something. Its full nutritional power is in your mouth and your taste buds are sending a myriad of passionate signals to the brain: hot, sour, bitter, sweet, strong. When you cook food, you tame it, de-claw it, rob it of savage vitality as well as its ability to renew and cleanse the body at a cellular level. It's the enzymes and other organic chemicals that explode on your palate to announce they are full of life renewing qualities. Raw foods are immediately absorbed by the body because of the presence of enzymes in the food. It is for the same reason that the nutrients in raw foods are so readily available to the body and are many times more easily digested by the body.

Cooked foods are a great deal of labor for the body to digest, absorb nutrients from and pass through. Deep fried foods pose the greatest difficulty in this regard.

Raw Foods essentially come pre-digested, meaning they are ready to be absorbed by the body and do not have to be digested. Cooked foods require enormous bodily resources, especially enzymes, to be digested.

People don't stop to consider what they are putting in their body because they are not educated on nutrition. Instead, sadly, we are conditioned. Conditioned to believe that if it comes out of a box, can or jar, it's okay to eat it, regardless if it contains chemical substances and preservatives we cannot even pronounce. Consuming soft drinks is not questioned because marketing has duped us into believing there couldn't possibly be anything wrong with putting something so profoundly acidic as a carbonated soft drink into our body. The nutritional panels on packages reflects the pitiful amounts of nutrients that are actually in processed foods. And that assumes the body is going to absorb those nutrients, which it has a lot of trouble doing if they aren't consumed with the enzymes that are found only in raw foods.

They must work five to seven times harder when digesting and converting cooked foods into nutrients that can actually be used by the body than when digesting raw foods. This fact needs no further elaboration other than to say that cooked foods simply have no place in the body. The digestive tract must call on metabolic enzymes to do its job. Our organs are strained and must work overtime to produce sufficient amounts of enzymes to help with the difficult task of digesting cooked foods.

Raw Foods Built the Immune System

Building the body's cells with raw foods naturally protects us from bacterial infections and viruses of every kind. It fortifies the cells in ways that only raw foods can because the human body, as well as all life on Earth, has been conditioned to receive its nutrients in that way for billions of years. However, highly processed foods first appeared in the 1930's. The rise of chronic disease of all kinds

Consumption of Animal Fat and Heart Disease

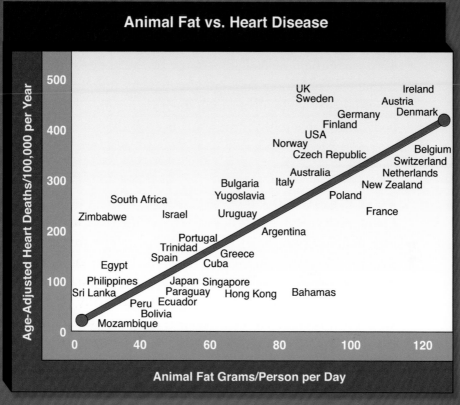

Animal Fat vs. Heart Disease

Taken from: Joel Fuhrman, M.D., *Eat to Live: The Revolutionary Formula for Fast and Sustained Weight Loss.* Boston: Little, Brown, 2003.

correlates precisely with the increased consumption of processed foods. Cancer is a perfect example of this. It has continued its meteoric rise since the 1930's until now one of every three people in the United States will get cancer in their lifetime. Switch to a raw food diet and disease will disappear from your life for good, or for as long as you remain a raw foodist.

Raw foods are never fattening. Regardless of the amount consumed, the body will assimilate the amount of nutrients it needs and expel the rest. People often believe that bananas, avocados and coconut are fattening, which they are not if they are consumed raw. Once cooked, processed or otherwise denatured, the fat, which has been chemically transformed, will undoubtedly deposit in the body. Fat deposited in the body this way is not a normal bodily process because denaturing food is not a natural process in and of itself. The body also stores them in such a way as to make them unavailable for use by the body except to burn the fat off. Fresh foods contain saturated fats, unsaturated fats and essential fatty acids, all of which the body requires. However, the body is also able to store these fats in its cells so it can use them as required by the body.

Learning to Find Satisfaction in Raw Foods

Hunger is a base instinct that is easily *satisfied* with cooked foods. The major reason for this is conditioning. The hypothalamus, the on/off hunger switch in the body, has been triggered and the cooked-foodist *feels full*. While the belly is indeed full, it is filled with substances that do not carry with them the enzymes that allow their nutrients to be immediately absorbed and utilized by the body. Instead, we force the body to work many times harder to absorb nutrients from the foods we consume because they are denatured. We strain our enzyme reserve. Other areas of the body become neglected, most importantly our immune system. This should be the real reason we call it the *common cold*. As we age, we deplete our enzymes reserves until we begin to call upon our metabolic enzymes to help digest our foods. The body strains ever harder to absorb nutrients. The digestive tract becomes ever more clogged because of the absence of crucial digestive enzymes whose presence helps keep it clean and flowing. Simply put, we should not put anything in our bodies other than substances that are pure nutrients, i.e., *raw foods*.

The thing most people want from eating is a *full* belly. They equate this with having fed their body and satisfied its need for nutrients. Many realize they have done nothing but turn off the hunger switch. A belly full of cooked food is slow moving if not stagnant, especially if it has not been *primed* with raw foods, such as a hearty salad, before their cooked food meal.

However, we can learn to truly satisfy our hunger pains without resorting to cooked foods.

Upon introducing someone to the raw food theory, many people, especially vegetarians, . . . proudly state that they eat a lot of steamed vegetables. Steamed vegetables are *not* at all acceptable because steaming kills the enzymes and therefore much of the nutritional potential of the food. It distorts the natural state of the food and therefore the original intent of the nutrients' effect on the body.

What You Should Know About Vegetarianism

Facts About Vegetarianism

- 6 percent of 8- to 18-year-olds say they never eat meat: 1 percent eat a vegan diet.
- 11 percent of 13- to 15-year-old girls and 9 percent of boys the same age say they never eat meat.
- More than 12 million people in the United States are vegetarians.
- 40 percent of people are flexitarians, i.e., sometimes eat vegetarian meals.
- Vegetarians are more likely to be female, single, low-income, and young.
- Nearly one-fourth of college students say that finding vegan meals on campus is important to them.
- People who eat higher amounts of fruits and vegetables have about one-half the risk of cancer.
- Lifelong vegetarians have a 24 percent lower rate of heart disease compared to meat-eaters. Vegans have a 57 percent lower rate.
- In one study, healthy volunteers who consumed a vegetarian diet (containing 25 percent of calories as fat, and rich in green, leafy vegetables and other low-calorie vegetables, fruits, and nuts) for two weeks had 25 percent lower cholesterol.
- Lacto-ovo vegetarians who eat a diet that is very high in fat and saturated fat may have a rate of heart disease similar to the general population.

- Vegetarians generally have a lower incidence of high blood pressure and a lower rate of type 2 diabetes.
- Vegetarians, especially vegans, have less incidence of obesity.

Meat and the Environment

- More than 10 billion animals are killed for food in the United States per year.
- A typical American meat eater is responsible for nearly 1.5 tons more carbon dioxide a year than a vegan.
- 260 million acres of U.S. forest have been cleared to create cropland to grow grain to feed farmed animals.
- Farmed animals are fed more than 70 percent of the corn, wheat, and other grains grown in the United States.
- Almost half the water and 80 percent of the agricultural land in the United States is used to raise animals for food.
- It takes 5,000 gallons of water to produce a pound of California beef.
- It takes five pounds of protein feed to create one pound of consumable chicken protein.
- Livestock in the United States produces about 30 times more excrement than humans. Human waste is processed in sewage systems, but most excrement from feedlot animals leaches into water.
- 55 percent of the antibiotics used in the United States are fed to livestock.
- Tens of billions of chickens produced today never go outdoors.

Pasture-Raised Animals

- The natural diet of ruminant animals—hooved animals like cows and sheep—is grass. Most factory-farmed animals eat grains. As of yet, a cow's digestive system has not evolved to support this new diet.
- Animals fed grain in a factory farm are more susceptible to health problems like acidosis, rumenitis, liver abscesses, bloat, and feedlot polio.

- The low-fiber grain diet allows harmful bacteria to proliferate in cows.
- Grass-fed beef has four times the vitamin E than grain-fed beef, a third less fat, and two to four times the omega-3 oils.
- Grazed land has environmental benefits over cultivated cropland, including: 53 percent better soil stability, 131 percent more earthworms, less nitrate pollution of groundwater, and improved stream quality. Moderately grazed land also produces greater wildlife diversity.
- The grasses in a pasture helps absorb carbon dioxide from grazing animals.

What You Should Do About Vegetarianism

There is no one correct way for everyone to eat. Smart, kind people who have given much thought to the issue of what to eat can easily disagree on whether it is right or good to eat meat. It is a very personal issue and there are many different reasons why someone might choose one diet over another. For one person, environmental issues might be the most important factor. For another, animal rights would be a deciding factor. Others make decisions based on health reasons or what their friends and family are eating. Some do not give much thought to the issue and just eat what tastes good.

There is no one right answer for everyone, but that does not mean you cannot advocate a particular way of eating to let other people know about its benefits.

Start with Your Own Diet

The best place to start is with yourself and the first step is to become well-informed. Whether you opt for a vegetarian or meat-based diet, study sample meal plans in books or on the Internet to make sure you are getting the right nutrients. For example, a vegetarian who eats a lot of processed foods and vegetarian junk foods is not eating a healthy diet. Figure out how you want to eat. Sometimes what you think you want to eat and what actually works for your body might be different. It is okay to experiment with different types of diets to see what works best with your body. Your best result will probably be something that incorporates lots of fruits and vegetables, whole grains, and lean protein sources. A good, balanced diet will keep your physical, mental, and emotional energy at an even keel throughout the day.

Talk to Your Family

The next step is to talk with your family about your choices. If you are a budding vegetarian in a meat-eating family or a meat-eater in a vegetarian family, your family may be concerned about your decision. The best way to put them at ease is to show them that you have really thought about the issue and taken care to educate yourself. Vegans, for example, might reassure their parents that they are meeting their protein needs and are aware of how they might need to supplement their diets. Offer to take over cooking some of the meals to showcase the delicious and healthy options in your diet. If you present your case in a clear, reasonable manner and show your family that you can thrive on your diet, your example might even persuade others to do the same.

Talk to Your Friends

If you adopt a diet that people are not familiar with, you may get some questions. Answer the questions honestly and fully, without being preachy or judgmental. Just as a vegetarian does not want to be hassled to try a piece of steak, a meat-eater does not want to be harangued about eating a hamburger. A polite and respectful attitude is best. And again, sharing delicious food from your diet is always a good way of helping people to appreciate it. You might find others who will not agree with you. If no one around you shares your beliefs, head to the Internet. No matter what your food preference, there are going to be several communities dedicated to that lifestyle.

What to Do

The first and easiest thing to do is to talk about food and where it comes from. If you have to give a report at school, make it on something you care about like sustainable farming, raw foods, or the value of meat in a diet. Write an editorial for your school paper or local paper advocating your point of view. Read books about food and where food comes from and, if someone seems interested, talk to them about it. If your school cafeteria is not offering the kind of lunchtime options that you want, lobby the school administration. If you want, say, more sustainably farmed meat incorporated in the school menus, talk to the PTA and the principal and find out what you can do to help make it happen.

Lobby Businesses

See if your family is willing to support your choices with their shopping habits. Perhaps they will be willing to seek out locally raised meat or will go with you to a local farmers market. You can also ask the managers at local supermarkets to stock the kinds of foods—such as humanely raised beef—that you want to see in their stores.

You can also organize letter-writing campaigns to supermarket chains, restaurants, and food manufacturers in support of your dietary choices. You could write to a fast food chain, for example, asking them to offer more vegetarian options. Support businesses whose products are in line with your preferences.

Volunteering and More

Volunteering is another good way to support your beliefs. If you are concerned about cruelty to animals, find a local chapter of a group such as PETA (People for the Ethical Treatment of Animals). Work at a local farm that raises animals on pasture. Help a farmer work a booth at a farmers market and talk to customers about food. Raise money for your favorite causes.

You can start a formal activist group at school or perhaps a more casual group that takes on an occasional action. Your group can make a presentation at an assembly, perform a skit in a school talent show, or stage creative demonstrations. Having a sign-up booth at school functions is a way to get new members and to let people know about your group and its beliefs.

If starting a group or even writing a letter seems too daunting, feel free to start simply by changing your own diet. Little changes can make a big difference.

ORGANIZATIONS TO CONTACT

American Vegan Society (AVS)
56 Dinshah Ln., PO Box 369, Malaga, NJ 08328
(856) 694-2887 • fax (856) 694-2288
Web site: www.americanvegan.org

The society is a nonprofit educational organization dedicated to teaching a compassionate way of living that includes veganism. It hosts vegan events and conferences and the Web site offers information about veganism. The AVS publishes the quarterly magazine *American Vegan*.

Coalition for Non-Violent Food
c/o Animal Rights International
PO Box 1292, Middlebury, CT 06762
(203) 598-0554
e-mail: info@ari-online.org • Web site: www.ari-online.org

The coalition is a program of Animal Rights International. It seeks to reduce animal suffering by reducing the consumption of animal products, as well as by refining animal agriculture methods. The Web site offers information on past and current campaigns as well as links and resources.

Compassionate Cooks
PO Box 18512, Oakland, CA 94619
(510) 531-2665
e-mail: info@compassionatecooks.com
Web site: www.compassionatecooks.com

Compassionate Cooks seeks to empower people to make informed food choices and to debunk myths about vegetarianism and animal rights. It offers cooking classes, recipes, resources, workshops, lectures, articles, and essays. The organization produces the Vegetarian Food for Thought podcast, a vegetarian cooking DVD, and the cookbook *The Joy of Vegan Baking*.

Compassion Over Killing (COK)
PO Box 9773, Washington, DC 20016
(301) 891-2458
e-mail: info@cok.net • Web site: www.cok.net

COK is a nonprofit animal advocacy organization based in Washington DC. COK focuses on cruelty to animals in agriculture and promotes vegetarianism as a way to build a kinder world. It publishes the magazine *Compassionate Action*.

Eat Wild
PO Box 7321, Tacoma, WA 98417
toll free: (866) 453-8489 • fax: (253) 759-2318
e-mail: fro@eatwild.com • Web site: www.eatwild.com

Eat Wild provides information about the benefits of raising animals on pasture. It links consumers with local suppliers of all-natural, grass-fed products and provides a marketplace for farmers who actively promote the welfare of their animals and the health of the land. The Web site offers articles that promote the benefits of grass-fed animals.

International Vegetarian Union (IVU)
Parkdale, Dunham Rd., Altrincham WA14 4QG,
United Kingdom
fax: 44 161 9269182
e-mail: chair@ivu.org • Web site: www.ivu.org

IVU, founded in 1908, is a nonprofit organization dedicated to promoting vegetarianism throughout the world. Its main objectives are to encourage the formation of vegetarian organizations and cooperation between them, promote vegetarianism, and encourage research into all aspects of vegetarianism. It publishes a monthly newsletter, *IVU Online News*.

Jewish Vegetarians of North America
49 Patton Dr., Newport News, VA 23606-1744
(410) 754-5550
e-mail: imossman@bluecrab.org • Web site: www.jewishveg.com

The Jewish Vegetarians of North America advocate a vegetarian diet as a way to follow Jewish teachings. The Web site offers a free downloadable CD, "Judaism & Vegetarianism," the book *A Case for Jewish Vegetarianism*, and a free online course on Judaism and vegetarianism.

North American Vegetarian Society (NAVS)
PO Box 72, Dolgeville, NY 13329
(518) 588-7970.
e-mail: navs@telenet.net • Web site: www.navs-online.org

The NAVS is a nonprofit educational organization dedicated to promoting the vegetarian way of life. Since its inception, it has organized and sponsored annual vegetarian conferences including two world events. NAVS publishes the magazine *Vegetarian Voice*.

People for the Ethical Treatment of Animals (PETA)
501 Front St., Norfolk, VA 23510
(757) 622-7382 • fax: (757) 622-0457
e-mail: info@peta.org • Web site: www.peta.org

PETA is the largest animal rights organization in the world. PETA focuses its attention on stopping cruelty to animals on factory farms, in laboratories, in the clothing trade, and in the entertainment industry. It works through public education, cruelty investigations, research, animal rescue, legislation, special events, celebrity involvement, and protest campaigns. It publishes the magazine *Animal Times*.

Raw Network of Washington
1037 NE 65th St., Suite 210, Seattle, WA 98115-6655
(206) 923-8908 • e-mail: info@rawwashington.org
Web site: http://rawwashington.org

The mission of Raw Network of Washington is to increase public awareness of the benefits of the raw/living foods lifestyle. It hosts community events and offers a message board and information about a raw foods diet on its Web site. The site also has information about things relating to raw foods, including farmers markets, books, films, retreats, and raw food products.

Sustainable Table
c/o GRACE
215 Lexington Ave., Suite 1001, New York, NY 10016
(212) 991-1930 • fax: (212) 726-9160
e-mail: info@sustainabletable.org
Web site: www.sustainabletable.org

Sustainable Table promotes the sustainable food movement, educates consumers on food-related issues, and works to build community through food. To help people support sustainable food, the organization offers teacher guides, articles, and plans for school gardens, and the Web site has a feature that allows users to enter their zip code to find nearby locally produced food.

Vegetarian Resource Group (VRG)
PO Box 1463, Baltimore, MD 21203
(410) 366-8343 • fax: (410) 366-8804
e-mail: vrg@vrg.org • Web site: www.vrg.org

VRG is a nonprofit organization "dedicated to educating the public on vegetarianism and the interrelated issues of health, nutrition, ecology, ethics, and world hunger." The Web site offers information on all facets of vegetarianism including recipes and nutrition and has a special section for kids and teens. The organization publishes the *Vegetarian Journal*, and sells books, pamphlets, and article reprints.

BIBLIOGRAPHY

Books

Victoria Boutenko, *12 Steps to Raw Foods: How to End Your Dependency on Cooked Food*. Berkeley, CA: North Atlantic, 2007.

Barbara Kingsolver, *Animal, Vegetable, Miracle: A Year of Food Life*. New York: HarperCollins, 2007.

Judy Krizmanic, *A Teen's Guide to Going Vegetarian*. New York: Puffin, 1994.

Erik Marcus, *Meat Market: Animals, Ethics, and Money*. Ithaca, NY: Brio, 2005.

Marion Nestle, *What to Eat*. New York: North Point, 2007.

Stephanie Pierson, *Vegetables Rock! A Complete Guide to Teenage Vegetarians*. New York: Bantam, 1999.

Michael Pollan, *In Defense of Food: An Eater's Manifesto*. New York: Penguin, 2008.

———, *The Omnivore's Dilemma: A Natural History of Four Meals*. New York: Penguin, 2006.

Peter Singer and Jim Mason, *The Way We Eat: Why Our Food Choices Matter*. New York: Rodale, 2006.

Bob Torres and Jenna Torres, *Vegan Freak: Being Vegan in a Non-Vegan World*. Colton, NY: Tofu Hound, 2005.

Periodicals

Reed Albergotti, "The 247 Lb. Vegan," *Wall Street Journal*, January 25, 2008.

Mark Bittman, "The Meat of the Matter," *Dallas Morning News*, February 10, 2008.

Amy Culbertson, "'Flexitarian' Dining Means More Options on the Table," *Fort Worth Star-Telegram*, June 22, 2007.

Christine Lennon, "Why Vegetarians Are Eating Meat," *Food & Wine*, August 2007.

Liz Minchin, "Limit Meat Eating to Tackle Climate Change: Study," *Sydney Morning Herald*, September 13, 2007.

Katie Norton, "Buying Organic Is Meating Vegans Halfway," *Georgetown Voice*, January 31, 2008.

Erin Oliveri, "All Hail: Meat-Lovers Far from Inferior," *Northeastern News*, October 22, 2007.

Kim Painter, "Veganism Is Taking Root, but Is It Healthy?" *USA Today*, January 29, 2008.

Karen Robinson-Jacobs, "FDA Approval Means Cloned Meat Could Make It to Dinner Tables," *Dallas Morning News*, February 11, 2008.

Nancy Smith, "Better Beef," *Mother Earth News*, February 1, 2008.

Vrinda Walker, "Attitudes, Practices, and Beliefs of Individuals Consuming a Raw Foods Diet," *Vegetarian Journal*, April 2006.

Greg Wiseman, "Proper Nutrition Choices Still Important for Vegetarians," *Melfort Journal*, February 12, 2008.

Internet Sources

Sally Parrott Ashbrook, "How to Eat Vegetarian on the Cheap," Get Rich Slowly, February 2, 2007. www.getrichslowly.org/blog/2007/02/02/how-to-eat-vegetarian-on-the-cheap.

Amy Chen, "Organic Meat: Healthy Animals Make Healthy Humans," Supermarket Guru, February 10, 2002. www.supermarketguru.com/page.cfm/141.

Bruce Friedrich, "Humane Meat: A Contradiction in Terms," Huffington Post, July 31, 2007. www.huffingtonpost.com/bruce friedrich/humane-meat-a-contradict_b_58547.html.

Brenda Lau, "How I Went Vegan," Vegetarianteen.com, 2005. www.vegetarianteen.com/articles/brendalau.shtml.

Reed Mangels, "Vegetarian Nutrition for Teenagers," Vegetarian Resource Group, May 14, 2003. www.vrg.org/nutrition/teen nutrition.htm.

Katie Ransohoff, "Vegetarianism in Teens," Palo Alto Medical Foundation, November 2004. www.pamf.org/teen/health/nutrition/veggieteens.html.

Rick, "First Year Journal of a Raw Teen," Vegetarianteen.com, 2005. www.vegetarianteen.com/articles/rawrick2.shtml.

Valerie Schultz, "An Even More Inconvenient Truth," Bakersfield.com, October 8, 2007. www.bakersfield.com/opinion/columnists/valerie_schultz/story/253108.html.

Peter Singer, "The Ethics of Eating," Project Syndicate, June 2006. www.utilitarian.net/singer/by/200606--.htm.

Mark Sisson, "My Escape from Vegan Island," Mark Sisson's Daily Apple, May 22, 2007. www.marksdailyapple.com/vegan-island.

Carol Price Spurling, "The Ethics of Eating Meat," *Moscow Pullman News*, September 12, 2006. www.plumassignment.net/_docs/meateating.pdf.

Lisa Vickers, "Why Most Vegans Are Usually Stupid," Makin' Waves, August 18, 2006. www.makinwaves.org/2006/08/why_most_vegans_are_usually_st.html.

Stephen Walsh and Glynis Chapman, "A Recipe for Abundant Vegan Health," *Vegan*, Autumn 2001. www.vegansociety.com/articles/aut01recipe.htm.

Polly Wise, "Making Raw Foods Delicious: Cherie Soria and Living Light International," *Natural News*, January 23, 2008. www.naturalnews.com/022530.html.

INDEX

energy consumption from agriculture, 62

meat consumption in, 61

teen eating habits in, 72

V

Veenis, Gaia, 70

Vegans, 70–73

Vegetarian diet(s)

the environment and, 58–62

guide for teens, 25

is best way to help planet, 50–57

is key to good health, 15–20

is weapon against global warming, 47, 49

steps in switching to, 19–20

sustainably raised meat and, 63–69

teens and, 21–28

types of, 15

of Vegetarian Research Group, 75

Vitamin B_{12}, 18–19

Vitamin D, 18

W

Water

animal agriculture and, 45, 51

use for animal agriculture, 47

The Way We Eat (Singer and Mason), 31

Willett, Walter, 12

World Bank, 54

PICTURE CREDITS